PERGAMON RUSSIAN CHESS SERIES

Kasparov v Karpov 1990

Kasparov v Karpov 1990

by
Garry Kasparov, Efim Geller, Anatoly Lein and Viktor Chepizhny

Translated by
Ken Neat

PERGAMON CHESS
Member of Maxwell Macmillan Pergamon Publishing Corporation
OXFORD · NEW YORK · BEIJING · FRANKFURT
SAO PAULO · SYDNEY · TOKYO · TORONTO

UK	Pergamon Press plc, Headington Hill Hall, Oxford OX3 0BW, England
USA	Pergamon Press Inc, Maxwell House, Fairview Park, Elmsford, New York 10523, USA
PEOPLE'S REPUBLIC OF CHINA	Pergamon Press, Room 4037, Qianmen Hotel, Beijing, People's Republic of China
FEDERAL REPUBLIC OF GERMANY	Pergamon Press GmbH, Hammerweg 6, D-6242 Kronberg, Federal Republic of Germany
BRAZIL	Pergamon Editora Ltda, Rua Eça de Queiros 346, CEP 04011, Paraiso, Sao Paulo, Brazil
AUSTRALIA	Pergamon Press Australia Pty Ltd, PO Box 544, Potts Point, NSW 2011, Australia
JAPAN	Pergamon Press, 5th Floor, Matsuoka Central Building, 1-7-1 Nishishinjuku, Shinjuku-ku, Tokyo 160, Japan
CANADA	Pergamon Press Canada Ltd, Suite No 271, 253 College Street, Toronto, Ontario, Canada M5T 1R5

First English Edition 1991

Library of Congress Cataloging-in-Publication Data
Kasparov, G. K. (Garri Kimovich)
Kasparov v Karpov 1990 / by Garry Kasparov . . . (et al.);
translated by Kenneth P. Neat. — 1st ed.
p. cm. — (Pergamon chess series)
Contains full account, with deep annotations, of world chess championship match, New York-Lyons, 1990.
Includes index.

1. Chess — Tournaments, 1990. 2. Kasparov, G. K. (Garri Kimovich)
3. Karpov, Anatoly, 1951-   . I. Karpov, Anatoly, 1951-
II. Title. III. Series.
GV1455.K2618 1991   794.1'57 — dc20   90-24873

British Library Cataloguing in Publication Data
Kasparov, G. K. (Garri Kimovich)
Kasparov v Karpov 1990. — (Pergamon chess series)
1. Chess. Championships. Games
I. Title
794.157

ISBN 0-08-041110-X

**Distributed in the United States and Canada
by Macmillan Publishing Company/New York
866 Third Avenue, New York NY 10022. 212-702-2000**

Printed in Great Britain by BPCC Hazell Books, Aylesbury

Contents

Acknowledgement

The authors wish to acknowledge with extreme gratitude the contribution of Andre Reichmann to this book.

Mr Reichmann provided us with generous financial support in order that this book might be written. It was the original intention that he be more involved in the writing but his many business and personal obligations prevented his active participation. Consequently, his support was given solely out of his great love of chess.

His interest in the game is more than just a casual one. He is the 1985 United States Chess Federation "Golden Knights" Postal Chess Champion, which he completed in 1990 with the perfect score of 18-0. He received his FIDE Master title in 1988 and he has been a student of Grandmaster Anatoly Lein's for a number of years. His over-the-board schedule is currently light but he is participating in numerous correspondence tournaments.

Mr Reichmann is a highly successful financial markets trader – also a mind game – and is President of Lance Capital Inc., which conducts research on world economies and capital markets primarily for the purpose of trading.

It is Mr Reichmann's wish that chess be appreciated by the people of all nations and particularly by its children. He feels that the excitement caused by bringing the first half of the match to New York will help to do just that. Besides the enjoyment of chess as an art form, Mr Reichmann also believes that the study of chess – along with a good education – can contribute greatly to the development of the mind.

Mr Reichmann resides in New York City. He is married and the father of four young sons.

Foreword by the Analysts

We present here our analyses and game commentaries. For us this was an interesting but difficult job. On the one hand we were aiming for high quality, but on the other hand we were very restricted in time. Nevertheless we hope that our work will be read with interest. We have endeavoured to cover not only the chess aspect of the match, but also the human essence of our champions. We hope that through our chess language we have been able to show that they too are people.

In conclusion, we should like to express our sincere thanks to those who helped us in these difficult days. To Paul Lamford, whose cordiality and affability raised our spirits, and to translator and analyst Ken Neat, whose chess questions (which we awaited "in fear and trepidation") frequently stumped us, but enabled, we think, the book to be improved.

Efim Geller, Anatoly Lein

Regulations for the 1990 Match

In the majority of international events (including Candidates matches) the time limit now used is 40 moves in two hours, with a further 20 moves in one hour before adjournment. But in this World Championship match the old time limit was still in use: 40 moves in two and a half hours, adjournment after five hours' play, and 16 moves per hour thereafter. (The players' clock times, when available, are given in italics after the moves.)

The match was split between New York and Lyon, with twelve games due to be played in each venue. But in the event of one player gaining a substantial lead in New York, the number of games played there was to be reduced. Each player was entitled to claim up to three postponements.

The official prize fund for the match was three million dollars, five eighths to go to the winner and three eighths to the loser. In the event of a drawn match Kasparov would retain his title but the prize money would be divided equally.

Chief Arbiter for the match was the Dutchman Geurt Gijssen.

The Two Players' Teams

Each player had a whole team of seconds to help with his preparations, analysis of adjourned games, etc.

Kasparov's team (all from the USSR) comprised Zurab Azmaiparashvili, Sergey Dolmatov, Mikhail Gurevich, Giya Georgadze and Alexander Shakarov, with his mother, Klara Kasparova, acting as head of his delegation.

Karpov's team was headed by Nikolai Krogius, and also included Ronald Henley (USA), Lajos Portisch (Hungary), Andrey Kharitonov, Aleksey Kuzmin, Mikhail Podgayets and Igor Zaitsev.

The Match Through the Eyes of Garry Kasparov

This interview with Viktor Chepizhny was given specially for the book by World Champion Garry Kasparov, immediately after his new victory over Anatoly Karpov in their fifth match for the World Championship.

The match concluded literally a few hours before the New Year 1991. This must have been the most splendid New Year present for you?

Of course it was pleasant to greet the New Year this way, but this victory can in no way be called a present. It was won in a very hard battle. The further I go on, the more difficult it is to defend my title, and each new match becomes increasingly important. In this match we were risking different things. Karpov risked not winning yet another encounter at the highest level, while I could lose everything for which I had fought for ten years and held for the last five.

It is well known that the basis of your successes is deep and thorough preparation for each important event. For this new encounter with your 'perpetual' opponent you must have begun preparing long before the match.

Since this was already our fifth match, it could have been expected that the preparatory work done by both players would be of the highest quality. In addition, this match differed from the previous ones by there being a normal three-year interval. We finally had sufficient time to rest after the race which accompanied the four previous matches. Nevertheless, previous experience was taken into account and, multiplied by such an interval, it should have brought good results. I should straight away say that Karpov prepared for this match much better than ever before. This fact is important to note, since for the first time in my experience I had to contend with a better prepared opponent.

Why was Karpov able to prepare better? Because before the match itself he had to pass through a severe selection process. Playing three Candidates matches is a good form of training. This gives an undoubted

1

advantage, as I know from my own experience. One acquires form and self-confidence. Victories over strong opponents provide inspiration. One has an established team, working together for a year and a half in the same rhythm, with practised set-ups, well-considered plans and well-organised work.

By contrast, my team was assembled in parts essentially just before the match itself. Nevertheless, this cause should in no way be considered the main one. The enormous preparation experience which I have accumulated, and the ability to choose the correct strategic course, in which I have always been superior to Karpov, could have proved more weighty factors. Back in January 1990 I began planning my preparation, considering how to allocate my efforts, and where and with whom to carry out my training sessions. But there are events over which we have no control.

You have in mind the January events in Baku, as a result of which you not only broke off your first training session, but were also forced, together with your relations, to flee from your native town?

Yes, of course.

You were left without a home, and it is not hard to imagine all the problems which piled up on you. Did you nevertheless succeed in carrying out fully your intended preparation plans for the match?

To say that the preparation was not carried out fully would be an understatement. The sort of preparation which I am accustomed to seeing was altogether absent. Before each match for the World Championship I used to reckon that a hundred days of work were necessary. On this occasion I barely managed to scrape together sixty training days, but these were by no means those unclouded days of preparation on the banks of the Caspian Sea, which we had earlier. Pre-match concerns were closely interwoven with other vitally important problems. There was the enforced flight from Baku, and the necessity of seeing to my relatives, who ended up as refugees. There was also the general crisis in the country, and my involvement in political life. There were also upheavals with the match itself, which was divided between America and Europe, and training sessions held abroad. All this was very difficult and unaccustomed. The normal pattern of life was destroyed. And this before such a match! There was neither sufficient time, nor reserves of nervous energy, nor calmness. The only thing that I succeeded in doing was to outline the strategic course of the coming encounter, although only very approximately.

And what strategy did you plan?

On the whole the aim was for maximum complexity with both colours, to avoid giving Karpov any sort of respite. Thus there was a radical change in my approach compared with the previous matches, especially the last one in Seville, where reliance was placed on the white pieces, and with Black I played solidly and soundly. The choice of such a strategy largely resulted from impressions remaining from the previous match. There neither Karpov nor I achieved an appreciable advantage with the white pieces. I scored 3–2, and Karpov 2–1. Therefore it appeared that the past was likely to be repeated. Alas, the match demonstrated the fallaciousness of such an aim. And more important – for a long time the intended course prevented necessary corrections from being made in the match strategy during the match.

On what openings did you mainly pin your hopes?

As Black I chose two openings – the King's Indian Defence and the Grünfeld Defence – ultra-complicated, demanding the maximum concentration, a great amount of work, and thorough practical analysis. Unfortunately, here I was unable to achieve a high standard of preparation. With White, on the other hand, I managed to prepare excellently. And even before the match itself it became clear that White was bound to dominate. As was confirmed. In this situation it was essential to introduce significant changes in the 'Black' strategy, if not before the match, then at least during the course of it, in order if possible to have room for manoeuvre. But since in the pre-match period I was physically and psychologically tired, and in severe time trouble, I instinctively avoided adding to the amount of work. And therefore this amount began to be reduced. It was natural that everything 'superfluous' for Black, such as the preparation of quiet opening variations, came under this reduction. This was to leave its mark later, for example in the 23rd game. Instead of playing, in accordance with the situation, a quiet opening with my sights on a draw, I again rushed forward. And this direct initial aim, which, more importantly, was not in keeping with my level of preparedness, was the source of many of my problems in the match. With every game it was to become increasingly clear that it was not correct, since the white pieces, as in no other of our matches, were clearly dominant. And besides, to be frank, I did not imagine how well prepared my opponent would be.

During the match this quickly became evident.

Yes, but during the match everything is much more difficult to do. And there is another important factor, which I have already mentioned. I did not succeed in carrying out in full my preparation program, which had to be reduced to 60 days, and that with many breaks and distractions due to other things. It is quite obvious that when the time for preparation is reduced, the program itself also begins to be reduced, it is cut short. And therefore another incorrect step was taken, one which almost proved fatal. I wanted not only to play for complications with Black, but I even began avoiding theoretical duels, planning various irregular set-ups, deliberately going in for inferior positions, merely in order to avoid theory and maintain the tension. Tactics which are completely atypical of me, and in the given instance I stifled my own style of play. Usually Karpov used to avoid theoretical duels. And after all, my credo is to make the best moves. And now I myself went in for play more in accordance with Karpov's style, and to which he resorted, for example, in the 1985 match, when he was badly prepared. In general it was an attempt to plug the holes at the expense of deviating to one side.

And so your repertoire with Black proved highly unreliable.

It was not so much the repertoire that was to blame, so much as the insufficient preparation. I realised all this perfectly well, and it was for this reason that I decided to gather all my strength and attempt to crush Karpov at the very start of the match, by planning, so to speak, a 'blitzkrieg'.

And in general, to judge by the first few games, you had very real chances of achieving your aim. Especially if you had managed to win the 3rd game.

I simply did not have enough nervous energy. Had I managed to rest before the match for even a couple of weeks, it is quite possible that the 'blitzkrieg' would have succeeded. After all, in the first six games I could have gained three extra points. Of course, then it would have been a different battle, but even so, had I landed a series of blows at the start, I think it unlikely that Karpov would have held out.

The impression was that your physical condition too was not at its best. In my opinion, in a number of games in the New York half of the match you simply lacked strength in the fifth hour of play.

That's right. In order to be fully armed for a difficult and lengthy match, one must thoroughly prepare for it and rest well. My only normal preparation session came just before the match itself, in America, on the shore of the Atlantic Ocean. That is, a little more than a month in an entire year. In Spain I was simply coming to after the numerous unanticipated and adverse events which showered on me at the start of the year. But 30 days is a very short period, so as then to successfully conduct a gruelling three-month struggle. For the first time I was unable too to carry out purposeful physical preparation.

As in Zagulba?

Yes. Of course, an impression was left on the entire match by the fact that for the first time in ten years I was unable to carry out training sessions at my constant base at Zagulba near Baku. All my life I had regularly prepared in one place, in familiar surroundings. Daily runs along the shore of the Caspian Sea, intensive swimming, regular games of football and tennis. After such training I could withstand any amount of physical stress. And in one instant I was deprived of all this, to say nothing about the fact that I lost my home. All was destroyed, and I was completely unsettled. It was in view of all this that I intended to give my all at the start of the match, in order immediately to gain a decisive advantage. But when this did not succeed, depression set in, and I felt terribly tired.

It is good to begin a 'blitzkrieg' with White. But for the fourth time in these matches you had to play the first game with Black. Were you very upset by the result of the draw?

Of course I was upset. I will say why it is not very pleasant to play Black in the first game of a match. Essentially you have to play one game more as Black. In practice the 24th game falls out of the general scheme; it as though bears no relation to the match, since only the result is important. But in a long match the colour of the pieces with which you play the starting game is not so important.

As for the first game in the present match, as usual it was of an exploratory nature, and I deferred my determined attack until the second, 'White' game.

In your pre-match preparation, were you able to guess correctly your opponent's opening preparation?

It could be said that with Black neither player managed to guess correctly. I was guided by those variations that Karpov usually plays against the King's Indian and Grünfeld Defences. He did not play anything of the sort! Strictly speaking, everything that I prepared for the match with Black was not in fact used. The only exception was the 3rd game. But this was pure bluff! In all the remaining games I encountered variations for which I had not specially prepared. When I was playing White, on the other hand, a great surprise awaited Karpov. He of course expected 1 e4, but can hardly have expected that this move would be the main one. In fact the only one! The 24th game does not count! And in general he was unable to find any counter to this. In one game he played Petroff's Defence, and in the opinion of the observers he quickly equalised (in my opinion, there too he stood badly). Moreover, he did not 'poke his nose' into the main variation of Petroff's Defence. He did not once play the Caro-Kann Defence, realising perfectly well that, if I was regularly playing 1 e4, I would certainly have been very well prepared for this opening. In general, Karpov had to defend on Spanish lines, but the results turned out badly for him. To my achievements I would also assign my preparation of the Scotch Game, the employment of which Karpov, of course, did not expect. The 14th game in this ancient opening saw a new set-up, which enlivened and modernised this opening. And as a result Karpov ended up in a poor position.

But were there no similar surprises on Karpov's part?

Why not? In the very first game he quite unexpectedly employed the Sämisch Variation. When I and my trainers were preparing the King's Indian Defence, some of them thought that the Sämisch Variation would definitely not occur. This variation is very complicated, and often involves play on opposite flanks. I think that Karpov's choice of this variation was motivated by the fact that against it I play various lines, which means that I do not have a clear-cut repertoire. And in general this corresponds to the truth. In the initial game I chose some side variation and achieved an excellent game. The most interesting thing is that later, when my trainers and I began preparing in transit a reply to the Sämisch, in view of the favourable situation we decided to settle on a couple of deviations, which were later employed – in games 21 and 23. The quality of them does not require any commentary. In both cases Black's position from the opening was extremely dubious.

Why did you not repeat the opening of the 1st game?

The point is that in this variation White can castle long. This is the strongest continuation, which Karpov decided against employing in the initial game. But at the finish I am sure that this is what he would have chosen.

On what did you pin your main hopes with Black, the King's Indian or the Grünfeld Defence?

The King's Indian. Our reckoning was that Karpov does not play King's Indian set-ups very confidently. In general the character of the play in the King's Indian Defence, where Black has his chances, is to my taste. But Karpov found a splendid possibility: he did not close the centre with d4-d5. It will be remembered that once, in the 19th game, he did this, gained an advantage, and even so very nearly lost. But he managed to avoid such positions, by finding a variation in which it is difficult for Black to gain active counterplay. Except for the 11th game, in which White could have played more strongly.

You must be pretty 'sick and tired' of your constant and well-studied opponent. Did he not appear in this match in a capacity which was new to you?

He did and, I think, not to me alone – he played in a new manner. Since 1984, when our 'unlimited' duel began, both our styles have evolved. But whereas I, it is said, have added to my style something from the Karpov arsenal, he, it would seem, has altogether changed his playing manner. That high-quality play, based on profound opening preparation, which I have professed and which Karpov has criticised in every way possible, he has now taken up. The games from the match testify: Karpov has tacitly acknowledged the superiority of this playing style. Thus the argument between the two trends of chess development – technical and creative – has concluded in favour of the latter.

On this occasion Karpov did not ignore theoretical preparation?

He never ignored it. But for this match he was prepared better than ever before. And most important, he was not just fundamentally prepared for a theoretical battle, but this preparation was closely coordinated with a strategic course. Also, it was aimed at interesting creative positions. It should be noted that in this match there were hardly any technical positions. Karpov completely rejected his usual style of squeezing points out of simple technical positions. He went in for a different, full-blooded and complicated type of play. And this came as a complete surprise to me.

Indeed, in a number of games he was the initiator of active play.

And this happened quite often. It is another matter that he found complete agreement on the part of his opponent, since I too happily went in for complications, for a battle. And it was largely thanks to this that the match proved so interesting and entertaining, perhaps the best of all the five. Of course, one could complain about the large number of mistakes, which was a most striking feature. But mistakes have always occurred in matches for the World Championship, and this match was no exception. But anyone who takes the trouble to analyse carefully the games from the match will be able to appreciate their true worth.

In the theoretical sense the match proved especially fruitful. This is immediately apparent. There were innovations in abundance.

The theoretical results of the match will undoubtedly exert a great influence on the development of modern opening theory. This is the result of qualitatively new and profound preparation. I think that the variations demonstrated by both players in the match were notable for their very high level. In this respect too our fifth match surpassed all the previous ones. Karpov had some serious achievements – his set-up against the Grünfeld Defence, the move order chosen, deserves the highest evaluation. The set-up against the King's Indian with ♗e2 and ♗e3 is exceptionally unpleasant for Black. Much in it remained off-stage, but my trainers and I analysed it a great deal, so that we can evaluate it at is true worth.

I in turn landed some serious blows at Black in the 'eternal' opening – the Ruy Lopez. The move 19 f3, for example, in the 2nd game, the 18th game in general, and the 20th game. Although I did not clearly win the Spanish epic in the theoretical sense, since the opening evaluations in certain games were nevertheless not altogether clear. But in general a new type of position was tested, very complicated and interesting, in which I felt much more confident than Karpov.

But the results of the Spanish clashes were catastrophic for the Challenger. How do you explain this?

The whole point is that the resulting positions were clearly not to Karpov's taste. These are positions where the best move has to be found, which he does not particularly like.

Why then did Karpov persistently go in for these positions?

Perhaps because he had planned the same strategic course as I had. Karpov was attracted to these positions by a simple fact: three results are possible! He too wanted to win as Black, reckoning that with White I might overstep the mark, and he would gain chances of winning. Before the start of the match he evidently did not greatly believe in a favourable outcome, and therefore he thought that such chances with Black had to be exploited. It was another matter that he ended up in positions which objectively are more in accordance with my character than his. It should be mentioned that he employed the sharp Zaitsev Variation in games 2, 4, 20 and 22, i.e. either at the start of the match, when everything could still be repaired, or at the end, when he no longer had anything to lose. In the middle of the match he employed a more solid variation, which must be considered safe for Black. Those paths by which modern theory promises White an advantage in this variation apparently do not give anything. I have studied them long and carefully. But in games 12 and 18 I employed a set-up which may altogether refute the entire variation.

Do you think that Karpov planned to play for three results even before the match? Was that his aim?

Undoubtedly! The 2nd and 4th games indicate this. Especially the 4th – for three results. Karpov took a chance, and acted like a gambler. He either underestimated the fact that I play these positions better than he does, or he deliberately ignored this. I think that all this was a result of an analysis of our previous encounters, where I avoided risks, especially in Seville, where even as White I aimed to 'dry up' the play. As is evident, he too drew incorrect conclusions from the previous match. We based our analyses on previous material, but to a great extent did not take account of the evolution of styles that both have undergone during the preceding three years. It would seem that we both overlooked the changes which had occurred with us. I began playing much more sharply, more confidently going in for complications. Karpov too began playing more actively, and was prepared to take risks, not at all as in 1987.

Why did certain observers accuse Karpov at the start virtually of cowardice?

At the start Karpov was indeed afraid. But it should not be forgotten that he encountered a mass offensive. I was eager for a 'blitzkrieg', and played with great vigour, boldly and strongly.

Nevertheless, Karpov stood his ground.

Karpov lost only one point, and indeed got away with a fright. As I have already said, I did not have sufficient energy, and I used up much of my reserves without achieving a lot. My lead proved precarious and short-lived. My defeat in game 7 was the consequence of overall unpreparedness. At the start I used up too much strength, I gave my all. And a natural decline set in. Largely of a psychological nature. The further the match went on, the clearer it became that my preparation with Black did not stand up to any criticism. Each odd-numbered game, when I had the black pieces, became a difficult test. In game 7 I chose some side variation. And when at last I managed more or less to repair the position – "saved, thank God!" – that went and happened. This defeat had a clear psychological cause: it was due to the fact that I had not managed to build on my success at the start.

And how did things go with your psychological preparation?

Not badly on the whole. True, I did not manage to rid myself of my chief defect: I mobilise myself only when I stand badly. This is well known, and was confirmed by our last match.

An interesting detail: throughout the many years of my rivalry with Karpov, I have never won against him two successive games, with the exception of games 47 and 48 from the first match. At critical moments I have gathered myself and played much more strongly. But to maintain a state of complete battle-preparedness throughout an entire match is a very difficult problem. Only at the start of the match and during its second, Lyon half did I play reasonably confidently. To a considerable degree my psychological instability was a reflection of my overall preparation.

In matches for the World Championship psychological stresses are inevitable. Over a period of three months of very difficult struggle you had to endure a number of unpleasant moments, experience doubts and disappointments, and exist in stressful situations. How did you succeed in relieving these stresses?

All this, of course, had to be endured. I was disappointed when I was unable to transform my enormous playing advantage into a points lead at the start of the match. Doubts? One can never avoid doubts. After the first six games there began a difficult period for me, one which could have turned any player into a state of panic. I failed to win won positions, I miraculously managed to save positions which just before had been favourable. I understood why all this was happening, but it was not altogether clear how to overcome it. In general we lived with stresses. Fortunately, there were also many positive emotions. How did we relieve the nervous tension? With walks in the park: both in New York and in Lyon there was one nearby. Sometimes I ran, sometimes I played tennis. But to be honest, on this occasion inexcusably little attention was devoted to physical preparation. In the Lyon park there was also an excellent menagerie. This helped to distract and relax me. After the match, to the question by journalists "Did you have any parapsychologists?", Karpov mumbled something incomprehensible, but I replied: "I did! The stag and the wild goat which I fed every day on my walks."

What did you think of the appearance towards the end of the well-known sports psychologist Zagainov in Karpov's team?

I didn't think anything of it; this is a fact from his biography. And after all, he wasn't the only psychologist there. Aren't Krogius and Akimov also experts in this field? Perhaps Karpov needed them.

So there wasn't a psychologist in your team?

No, there wasn't. And not only was there no psychologist. For the first time my team had no chief trainer, such as Alexander Nikitin, who worked for many years with me.

Why did you part?

He himself left, without explaining the reasons. As he said in an interview: "Kasparov and I have parted without any fuss." Back in April I discussed with him the strategy for the forthcoming match . . . But he left, and I did not try to detain him. Perhaps he thought that he could no longer cope with the enormous tension that accompanies all World Championship matches, without exception.

At any event, I encountered a problem when there was not that person who would have headed our operational headquarters. My team was young. Although, almost all the trainers had worked with me at some time before: Zurab Azmaiparashvili and Sergey Dolmatov in Seville, and Mikhail Gurevich in Leningrad. Alexander Shakarov has been helping me since my childhood days. And only Giya Georgadze was a 'new recruit'. In short, I myself had to carry out the functions of chief trainer. Organise the work of the trainers, allot concrete tasks, think up new ideas, and also . . . play the match! Such work was new for me, and I do not think that I was very successful with it. The trainers conscientiously did their work. True, not all tasks were within their powers. The theoretical duel took place as though on foreign territory. The openings which had to be analysed were ones which practically none of my trainers play. They had to delve into positions about which for a long time they only had a very rough impression. In addition, three of them are strong grandmasters. They frequently approached the evaluation of this or that position from the practical viewpoint: "It is playable!" But I have a completely different approach. Even so, often they were able to 'persuade' me. As, for example, in game 23. Yes, a playable position was reached. But I am accustomed to finding the best continuation. And if I know that in a certain continuation the opponent is assured of an advantage, I do not go in for it. My colleagues think that this is possible. This is by no means a reproach, but demonstrates the different approach to chess which I had to encounter. It was for this reason that we were unable to overcome the unfavourable developments in parts of the theory battle. And in general, in opening preparation we were unable to gain superiority over Karpov, or even to achieve his level. On this occasion the fate of the match was decided at the board.

How then did you succeed in outplaying such a formidable and well-prepared opponent?

I simply played better chess than he did. In every stage of the game. The last phase in which I managed to outplay Karpov was in the practical endgame. There, where it was necessary to squeeze the maximum out of the position, I did so. In three adjourned games, where I might have gained only half a point, I picked up two. I had one hopeless ending, one difficult and one better. It was here that the fate of the match was decided. I outplayed Karpov in the practical endgame.

Karpov picked up points in positions where I made a mess of things. He simply exploited all the chances that I gave him.

There was one further fact that led to his defeat – constant time trouble. In total, Karpov spent four and a half hours more on his moves than I did. In other words, he essentially played two games more. He clearly had insufficient time, perhaps on account of his age. Regular time trouble is a warning signal. He was all the time trying to play more quickly. Incidentally, this was one reason why he constantly played the Ruy Lopez – 15-20 moves can be made in a few minutes, on auto-pilot. And yet by move 30 he would already be running short of time.

Would you like to name the games from the match which you consider the best, your own and your opponent's?

Of my own – games 2, 18 and 20. I was very happy with them. Game 3 could have been a brilliant one. That was real pity!

Karpov too had a number of good games – the 17th and 23rd, for example. In the 14th there were many mistakes, but what a fighting and interesting game! Game 4 was equally good. All very worthy games.

Why did defence triumph so often?

The point is that, as is known, the attacker expends some three times more energy than the defender. In order to win, you have to give your all. And neither player shone as regards reserves of strength and nervous energy. Besides, we neither of us forgot about caution.

Apart from this, you were quite often let down by your obvious impatience, by striving to get at the opponent's king as quickly as possible, even in those positions where there were quiet, purely technical ways of realising a great advantage. Evidently this was also a consequence of your incorrect strategic approach?

Not only. In the middle of the match there was a prolonged series of games ... without a win for me. This seriously unnerved me. It is this that explains why I sometimes threw myself at the opponent. But then, is not attack the quickest way to win?

Alas, it often turns out that this way by no means leads to a win. Looking back, would you not admit that your 'blitzkrieg' strategy was incorrect?

One strategy is no better and no worse than any other. Everything is decided by preparation. Given the form I was in during the match, any strategy would have had its drawbacks.

Grandmaster Krogius wrote in one of the newspapers that you change your trainers "in order to obtain new ideas from them".

It is well known that on the whole my trainers obtain new ideas from me. Therefore that which Krogius says is justified for Karpov, whose team he headed in the first half of the match. There the changes are indeed for the obtaining of new ideas. This has been widely known since the time of Karpov's matches with Korchnoi. My trainers can confirm that out of every ten new ideas used in this match, nine came from me. Moreover, even during the resumption of adjourned games I all the time followed paths which I myself had planned. This was especially apparent in the 8th game, where I was able to save a hopeless practical ending.

Was the atmosphere in your team all right? Were there any conflicts?

The atmosphere was friendly, better than in previous matches. There were no conflicts even at the most difficult moments.

But were there any complaints by your trainers?

There were some, of course. But, as they say, winners are not judged. Having won the match, it would not be appropriate to talk about complaints.

But how did the trainers relate to your mistakes?

With tolerance. They believed that all the same I would win, since they considered me to be clearly stronger than Karpov. This also left its mark on their work; their advice was not always sufficient for the situation in question.

Did it come as a surprise to you that the Hungarian grandmaster Lajos Portisch joined the Karpov team?

Yes, I learned of this only just before the match. It is with his appearance in the opponent's team that I associate Karpov's qualitatively new level of preparation. I think that the best opening set-ups which Karpov employed with White were prepared with the help of Portisch.

Which, for example?

Both against the King's Indian and against the Grünfeld. Firstly, they are part of his opening repertoire, and secondly, he provided that supply of fresh ideas which Karpov's former trainers were unable to provide. After all, I know them well.

So, the 'blitzkrieg' did not turn out as hoped. But nevertheless the start succeeded, you seized the lead, and held the initiative . . .

The fact that the planned assault did not succeed greatly upset me. I realised that the match would inevitably enter a phase of prolonged struggle. And after my defeat in game 7 there began a prolonged crisis, which was aggravated by the dramatic 8th game. The section from games 7-9, when I was completely out of sorts, was the most difficult. I conducted the 8th game quite well, and achieved a strategically won position. It only remained to make a few precise moves for it to be completely won. I did not make them. Then in time trouble I practically lost this game which had been going so well. And it was only by a miracle and by a terrific concentration of will and all my strength that I managed to save a hopeless ending.

It seemed that, had you not saved this adjourned game, where to the surprise of many you chose tenacious but passive defence, which is not at all in your style (but which was evidently the best solution), you could have cracked.

In general that is how one loses three games in a row. But even so the position was not an easy one. In game 9 I was again a hair's breadth away from defeat. In the 10th game Karpov avoided a fight, and in the 11th I employed a very interesting innovation – I sacrificed the exchange in a well-analysed position, sacrificed quite correctly. The result was a very pretty game. And in game 12 I gained a great advantage, but was unable to exploit it, although the position was typically 'mine'. The switching of the queen to the kingside, closer to the enemy king, was very obvious. And the fact that I did not go in for this continuation shows that at that moment I did not have the required mood or self-confidence.

This game set the seal on the New York half of the match: 6-6. Did you very much want to achieve a winning score in America?

Of course, in America I have many friends, and I felt that the public largely supported me. But it did not happen. And in general, rightly so.

Even so, this was a surprise for many, and also for you yourself.

Frankly speaking, after the 8th game I was not averse to the level score being maintained until the break. After all, there was a real danger of my cracking up and losing. I was already aiming for the break, in order to rest and use it for further preparation.

On the other hand your American friends were undoubtedly distressed that the battle had been so difficult for you. But not for a minute did they have doubts about your overall victory.

They probably were distressed. But Americans are practical people.

They realised that the main thing was to win the match. And about this they did indeed have no doubts.

The organisers divided the match into two parts. But how, into what stages, was it divided by the course of the battle itself? What was its inner drama?

The start of the match was the first six games, that stage in which I had hoped to put my 'bloodthirsty' ideas into practice. Then the stormy 7th and 8th games. The conclusion of the New York half. Then the Lyon half – essentially a new match, where each player used the experience of the preceding part and the new preparation carried out during the two-week break. True, the 13th and 14th games were to some extent a continuation of the first twelve. I could still not get away from the course of the preceding struggle, but I already felt that, despite isolated strategic mistakes, I was improving, and regaining form.

Probably it would be correct to regard the phase from games 7-14 as the second stage of the match struggle, the 7th and 8th as the start of this stage, and the 13th and 14th as its conclusion. The 15th-17th games, which provoked a crisis, stand apart. In the 15th Karpov gained a great advantage, but in the end he almost lost it. In the 16th I broke his resistance. Yes, the following game, the 17th, I lost. But the main thing was that at last that depressing series of draws had been broken.

I lost the 17th game in one move. I saw many more dangers than anyone else in this position. But because all my attention was occupied with these mythical, as it turned out, dangers, I overlooked the real danger. And just as undistinguishedly as in the 7th game, I lost in one move. One blunder, and the whole game was gone. In addition, an opening crisis had arisen, since these positions did not appeal to me.

You have failed to notice one interesting regularity: I lost every third game played with a particular opening. Three King's Indians – the third I lost; three Grünfelds – the same, and then three more King's Indians, and again a loss in the third. That was the regularity.

Why did you not notice this strange regularity earlier and change openings, if only in game 23?

I noticed it. But the 23rd game was a special case. And the 17th concluded the crisis stage of the match; the event was entering the finishing straight. Strangely enough, after this defeat I came to life and began playing strongly. In the next three games I had an overwhelming advantage. Objectively speaking, I should have won all three and concluded the match immediately.

Interestingly, it was precisely at that moment that, in his report on games 16 and 17 in a newspaper, I. Akimov 'prophetically' headed it: "He would seem to have cracked". He had in mind, of course, you.

The fate of the match was indeed decided then, but by no means in favour of his protégé. The defeat itself in game 17 was unpleasant, but the trend was already established: I was outplaying my opponent. My offer of a draw in a superior position in the 19th game saved Karpov from a crushing defeat. Incidentally, the result of this offer was that in the 20th game Karpov took a risk and went for an open game. He probably took his decision under the influence of his psychologists, such as Akimov: "Come on, Tolya, he is ready!" And I was indeed ready . . . to win. It was in this mood that I went along to the 20th game. Perhaps in this position Black is not so bad, but what is important is the essence. The main thing is that all the white pieces are in the attack, and when I am in my normal form . . . Incidentally, Karpov became frightened when he sensed that I was in a fighting mood; he realised this from the speed with which I made my moves. I did not even work everything out to the end, but simply threw my pieces into the vicinity of the black king, and the attack developed of its own accord.

And before that there was the 18th game, in which Karpov employed a new plan. He made the opening moves very quickly. But I think that he was not completely confident about his prepared variation. His intuition did not let him down: in his preparations he overlooked 21 ♕c4!.

How could this have happened?

It is very easy to make a mistake in analysis. I know how this happens. After all, apart from 14 ♗f4!, as occurred in the game, there was also a mass of other continuations, incidentally, also very dangerous for Black. Everything had to be looked at, but to analyse everything is impossible. In analysis 21 ♕d2 is made automatically. So as not to give up a pawn! It is only at the board that you begin to understand what is what.

You found the strongest move at the board without particular difficulty?

It is obvious enough. In analysis it is deeply concealed in a sideline. But in a concrete position it is not difficult to find. It was clear that, if I tried maintaining my extra pawn, it would mean opening up the enemy bishops and giving myself weaknesses. Whereas, as played, for the pawn I maintained my centre, left Black with a weakness at c7, blocked the enemy bishop and also gained several tempi. Here there wasn't a great deal to consider. This victory gave me confidence and, on the contrary, undermined Karpov's confidence in a successful conclusion to the match.

This could be seen from the way that he behaved, and from his replies when we analysed the position after the game. One has to give Karpov his due: even after this he battled tenaciously. He always battles to the end.

In this period of the match you were in good form, on an upsurge. On the other hand, you were well familiar with the competitive qualities of your opponent, and you realised that even in the most hopeless situation he would not resign without a fight. Why then was the last part of the match not so cheerful for you?

Because psychological pressure began to have its effect: "The match is coming to an end, the match is coming to an end!" And besides, the set-up chosen by me in game 21 was doubtful. I had to dodge about in a highly dubious position. Nevertheless, up to a certain point I did not play badly, then I made a mistake and gave Karpov a chance. The adjourned position was extremely difficult for me. Even now I do not know its correct evaluation. As Dolmatov said, this ending demonstrated human helplessness in the face of chess. The two teams spent a total of about twenty hours analysing the adjourned position, and still could not decide whether it was a draw or a loss. Incidentally, Karpov sealed the strongest move. I took a purely psychological decision: to follow the path which Karpov expected least of all, although another plan was objectively stronger. Karpov could not withstand the tension, ran short of time, and the game ended in a draw. Or more correctly, I gained a moral victory, which essentially set the seal on the match as a whole.

But then the deficiencies of my character again told. I could not force myself to play in the 22nd game. I even chose an opening which would force me to play. But I started playing properly only when I was faced with danger. And I even outplayed my opponent, obtaining chances a piece down. I should have exploited this chance and tried to end the match immediately. But instead of this I forced a draw. And subsequently I was punished for my equability.

In the 19th game, on account of enormous fatigue, I did not want to play on in a position with an obvious advantage, and I then had to save a difficult adjournment in the 21st. In the 22nd I did not fight, and the result was the 23rd, or more correctly, the 24th! The 23rd game – that was a story in itself.

The 23rd game was a psychological crisis, an anticlimax after the very difficult struggle. I had already retained my title for another three years. Had the score been equal, I would have found the strength. But I was winning 12-10 and I simply chickened out. Instead of playing something different, something new . . .

This is a well-known rule. When in the 1985 match I went along to play Karpov in the 24th game, I was ready to play the Grünfeld Defence. I wanted to change the solid Queen's Gambit for something more active, but Karpov helped me by playing 1 e4, and I employed the Sicilian Defence.

But now, when there was the chance to replace a risky opening with a more solid one, I did not take it. In Lyon I played a set-up prepared earlier. This set-up is a good one if you are losing by two points, but not the other way round. Firstly, it is positionally suspect. And secondly, it would be justified psychologically, if the opponent had something to lose and was obliged to be cautious. To crown everything, I was not ready for the solving of the difficult problems which I encountered, and I quickly lost. To be fair, it should be said that in this game Karpov played very strongly. In general I was justly punished, and had to suffer in the 24th game.

The 24th game has its own laws. In this, your fifth match, this truth was again confirmed?

It certainly was. The 24th game is always a special case. I said to my trainers: "I know how to win against Karpov with White, but I don't know how to play for a draw." It was decided to play solidly and reliably, and I chose a closed game.

For the first time in the match you avoided opening with the king's pawn. In the 24th game I expected a Scotch Game.

Do you remember the 14th? Can you imagine playing such a position in the 24th?! Even knowing that the position is objectively good? Besides, there are many other similar lines there, also double-edged. This opening is for a win! I could have played the Scotch in game 22. Perhaps I should have played it. And in general I did not have the right to play 1 e4 in game 24, for one simple reason: this move had brought me victory in the match, it had fulfilled its mission. This is a royal weapon! How could I use it, knowing that I wanted a draw?!

You said that you suffered in the 24th game . . .

That's right. I don't have to explain the psychological pressure on the players in the final game, on the result of which so much depended. Although I chose a solid opening, a quiet game did not result. After the opening I made a number of mistakes, not very noticeable, but Karpov gained serious chances of drawing the match, and all my life I would have had to bear the stigma that our match had been 'fixed'. Fortunately, both players have nerves. Karpov also went wrong several times, and then in time trouble he altogether lost his way. After gaining an enormous material advantage, I said to him: "I offer a draw from a position of very great strength!" He accepted my offer. I think that in this case the final score in the match was of no significance. For me it really finished after game 22.

As you yourself put it, in the 24th game you risked not only losing a significant part of the money prize, to say nothing of the million-dollar prize of the French jewellery firm 'Korloff', but you also risked being accused of a pact with your opponent regarding the final outcome of the match. As your ill-wishers thought, it should have ended in a draw by mutual agreement. This means that these absurd rumours, which flared up with particular strength after your offer of a draw in a better position in game 19, also reached you? How do you explain them?

This can be very easily explained. It was very tempting at one stroke to discredit both players, and me in particular. This is a reflection of the feelings that the chess elite harbour for me.

What provokes these feelings?

There is no reason to like a player who has an Elo rating of 2800. For nine years I have not lost a single event. How can this be endured? It was understandable when this was done by Fischer, a chess fanatic, who did not recognise anything other than chess. But I do a mass of other things, and I still outplay all the strongest grandmasters.

There are probably also other reasons. Spassky, for example, says that you have broken up the chess world.

I am creating a world of professional chess, I am trying to do that which chess rightly deserves. I do not know how quickly and successfully everything will go, but the program which I devised back in 1985 is now about to be implemented. This is not easy, and it encounters the resistance of the chess elite. As it is things are good for the leading grandmasters, they do not need changes. In the GMA my activity goes against the grain, because the creation of new tournaments signifies a rapid change of generations, i.e. the successful grandees will be evicted from the arena by young players much more quickly than they would like.

The chess world has changed greatly in recent years. In 1985 Karpov and I played for 72 thousand roubles, now for 3 million dollars. For this too I am not liked. Very much so! In 1972 Botvinnik accused Spassky of selling the match to Fischer for 100 thousand dollars. For him it was an unbearable thought that for his one defeat Spassky received more than Botvinnik received for all his victories taken together. History repeats itself. Now Spassky himself accuses me of having a pact with Karpov.

How do you picture professional chess?

A professional sport is one which pays for itself. It is a question of prizes in competitions, broad television coverage, the inclusion of chess in school curricula, everything that makes chess a prestigious form of human activity. What must be achieved is that it should be constantly on the television screens, so that it can enter every home and become the possession of millions of families. Then there will appear professionals, giving simultaneous displays, reading lectures, and teaching chess in schools and in clubs. And chess will become a field of human activity that will acquire prestige and respect throughout the world.

Your match provoked great interest among chess fans and undoubtedly played a great role in popularising the ancient game. Although, it will be remembered, after your second match certain experts predicted a lessening of interest in the battle of the two 'Ks'. And here we already have your 5th match. The same chief dramatis personae, but, it would seem, the fans confounded the forecasts once again?

Since the prize fund of the match has increased, it means that interest in it has also grown. One should not confuse the interest in the match in our country with that in the world as a whole. At the moment we have too many other problems to be bothered much about the match. In the West the interest in chess encounters at the highest level is undoubtedly growing. There is a simple but convincing capitalist indicator: they pay money, this means that it is interesting!

The time is not far off when a chess computer may interfere in the battle of super-grandmasters. Surely such a match would create universal interest!

Computer programs have achieved considerable successes. We know that some of them have already gained wins over grandmasters, including Karpov. But a serious battle at the top level is still a long way off. Not earlier than 1995. I know that many programmers are working in this direction, but it is not so simple, there are problems. For the moment I am sceptically inclined.

Even so, during your match with Karpov the problem arose of a computer helping in the analysis of the adjourned position in the 16th game.

During the match there was no such problem. It was thought up by Karpov and Akimov. This was exposed. All who worked with computers in the match mentioned this to the press. Even such well-known chess programs as 'Deep Thought' and 'Mephisto' were unable to find a win in the adjourned position from the 16th game. But in the future such a problem may arise. Computers are becoming increasingly powerful, and soon even such complicated endings will be within their capacity.

In principle, the framework of World Championship matches demands reconstruction. It is clear that there must be reforms. It is quite obvious that postponements should be eliminated. The match should be played on fixed days, so that television can plan precisely its coverage of the event. A 'black hole', such as that before the 22nd game, should not happen. A week's break in a match that was almost at an end! Again a technical postponement! And again to Karpov's advantage, because my team was already essentially demobilised; everyone was anticipating the end of the match. This gave an additional chance to my opponent.

Would it not be rather awkward without postponements? What if a player should fall ill?

If that occurred, it would be a tragedy. But experience has shown that postponements are not taken on account of illness. Normally during a match no one becomes ill. In professional sport there are strict rules.

Something has to be done about the adjournment of games. The result should be known on the same day. This is a professional approach. At the same time, this would exclude the interference not only of trainers but also computers.

At any event, the time for reforms is ripe. I think that this will have been the last match under the existing rules.

Champions do not choose their opponents. But whom would you like to meet in the next match? And what is the probability that the tradition will be continued, and the world will witness a sixth match between Kasparov and Karpov?

I, of course, would like to meet a 'fresh' opponent. This would be interesting in the creative sense, and psychologically, and as regards preparation. As for Karpov's prospects, it all depends on the mood in which he left Lyon. If he thinks that he has a chance of beating me, he will fight and he may successfully come through the new elimination cycle. In many aspects he is superior to the other candidates. At any event, anyone who wishes to stop Karpov will have to play very strongly. As yet it is not clear who can do this. The most dangerous opponent for Karpov is, I think, Boris Gelfand.

Is the circle of your future opponents so small? In that case you can already begin preparing for the 1993 match!

For the moment I am prepared to bet: these two against all the others.
And in what mood, in your opinion, did Karpov leave Lyon?
You would do better to ask him. But I think that it was in a sombre
mood. He realised better than others that he had conclusively lost the
match. I recall how, during our first unlimited match, one satirist wittily
called me a "long-playing record-player".* I was losing 5-0 at the time,
but I did not give up. And in the end I emerged with honour from this
difficult position. Karpov and I have played five matches, and he has not
won one of them. So that it is he who has turned out to be the "long-
playing record-player". True, he is consoled by the score in our decisive
games, where, in his opinion, my advantage is not so appreciable. But
here he includes those five wins, gained at the start of our first, unlimited
match, the result of which, incidentally, was annulled. But in the
succeeding five years he has nothing to be proud of. It would be good if
Karpov were to remember that throughout his entire career he has not
won a single match against a World Champion. So that he would do
better not to make any comparisons at all.

*Your confrontation with Karpov is widely known. But in this match you
pleasantly surprised everyone with your joint analysis of the games after
they ended.*
A chess game is a part of life, lived by the two players. The enormous
tension demands an outlet, some kind of release. Besides, this is a creative
process; it is interesting to find out what your opponent was thinking at
this or that critical point of the game, what he saw, and which of your
plans remained undiscovered by him. And so we renewed brief discussions
after the game, quite involuntarily. But this does not mean that our
personal relations have improved.

*The disparity of your views beyond the chess board hardly gives any basis
for forecasting a general improvement in your relations with Karpov in the
future. But the impression is that your confrontation in the political plane
has lost some of its sharpness.*
Simply I have moved ahead, onto a different level. And earlier too it
was not Karpov himself, but the organisations which stood behind him.
The territory on which we grappled has disappeared. The State Sports
Committee and the USSR Chess Federation no longer exist – for me
anyway. All that remains is our confrontation on the chess board.

---

* There is a play on words in the Russian, which could also be rendered as "long-playing
loser". (Translator's note)

But even so, did your match not have any political slant? A reminder of this was the colour of the flags under which you appeared. Initially your decision to play under the Russian tricolour did not provoke any particular protest on the part of Karpov the communist. At the opening ceremony he said that it was all the same to him under which flag you appeared. But then he evidently changed his mind.

It was simply that at first they did not know what to do. The Karpov delegation was awaiting instructions from Moscow. And when they backed down, the same decision was taken as was in its time in Baguio, when Korchnoi was forced to take down the Swiss flag, and simultaneously the Soviet flag was removed. And here they were so plagued by the presence of the Russian tricolour that they were also prepared to sacrifice their own, red flag.

Did you calmly accept this decision?

Well, formally they had right on their side. I had simply begun wearing the tricolour as a form of badge. My aim was to express a protest, to demonstrate my solidarity with the Russians, and not to create a scandal.

Were you not put out by the opponent's psychological attack at the opening ceremony? When suddenly, with the event already essentially under way, he suggested that the existing rules be changed, and in the event of a drawn match to play on to the first win.

Firstly, this was not a surprise. Secondly, the absurdity of these statements was so obvious to everyone that even Karpov himself felt uncomfortable. It is well known to everyone that he himself enjoyed privileges about which other World Champions did not even dream. Against me he had both the draw in hand and also a return match. Why if a match is drawn does the Champion retain his title? Because the Challenger has not defeated him. That is the tradition. If anyone had the right to object to this, it was certainly not Karpov. But logical arguments in discussions with him are simply superfluous. No, I reacted calmly to all these psychological tricks. And besides, no one took them seriously.

Possibly this was prepared by Doctor of Psychology Krogius, who for the first time was heading the Ex-World Champion's team, in order to try and unsettle you?

I don't know. Of what significance is it? These are already shadows from the past. Perhaps they were appearing for the last time.

For your victory in the match you were awarded a prize made by French jewellers – a diamond-encrusted monogram in the form of two interwoven letters 'K', the value of which was estimated at one million dollars. When *did you take the decision to auction it, so that the money gained could be given to the assistance fund for Armenian refugees from Baku?*

I took this decision after game 20, when winning the match became a reality. This match was against a person who represented the communist system. At the start of the year the Armenian people suffered a tragedy which was provoked by the communists. It was quite clear that this prize, symbolising my victory, should help the people who suffered at the hands of this system.

But to judge by Karpov's comments in the press, he is nowadays a great democrat.

Many have now changed their colours, and he is not the worst of them.

By nature you are a very active person. You probably feel restricted with the framework of chess. There is also politics, public activity, organisational work, literature, and a mass of other things. What then for you does chess represent?

I do indeed have many interests. But all this enables me to live life to the full. And chess . . . Chess is nevertheless the main thing. Everything that I have achieved in life has been in one way or another associated with chess. The experience accumulated in fierce chess duels, the atmosphere of struggle which has accompanied my entire path to the top in chess, the resulting battle-hardening; all this helps me in life to find the correct solutions in the most unusual situations, and to correctly forecast the future. Chess formed me as an individual. If one resorts to figurative comparisons: chess for me is like a trampoline – a leap up, and back, for a fresh charge of energy.

So you have no intention of giving up chess?

I do not see any reason why I should give up chess. At the board I feel confident enough, and my development reserves are not yet exhausted – I am only 27. Of course, to be victorious in competitions all the time and to regularly uphold my champion's title is not easy: it demands great effort and an enormous output of nervous energy. But I look to the future with optimism, and I am confident that in 1993, in the next match, I will uphold my title of the strongest chess player in the world.

GAME ONE   8 October

The initial game in a match at this level is normally of a testing, exploratory nature. The fact that the same opponents were meeting for the fifth time in a match for the World Championship was unlikely to change seriously the character of the struggle in the first game. Yes, Kasparov and Karpov have thoroughly studied each other, and even by the most insignificant outward signs they can determine the playing mood of their opponent and his general chess state. But this is obviously insufficient. A player has to become accustomed to the new surroundings, overcome the natural starting nervousness, get into the game, and most important – determine what sort of form he and his opponent are in. On the basis of this the players develop their strategy in the initial stage of the match.

But the most critical question concerning both players is this: what opening repertoire will the opponent have developed during his preparations for the match? The answer to this came as early as the third move. That evening, on the stage of the comfortable Hudson Theatre on Broadway, the premier of the sharp King's Indian Defence took place: this opening had occurred only once in the four previous Karpov-Kasparov matches. Karpov in turn gave as good as he got: he unexpectedly chose the Sämisch Variation. It became clear that, right from the start, both players were in a fighting mood.

Kasparov quickly gained an equal position, but went wrong on his 19th move. Then Karpov in turn missed a far from obvious chance to win material (22 ♖xe8+!), and although he did eventually win a pawn, it was in a position where this was of no significance.

And so, a reconnaissance in force!

Karpov-Kasparov
King's Indian Defence

1 d4   *0.00* ♘f6 *0.00*

2 c4   *0.00* g6   *0.00*
3 ♘c3   *0.00* ♗g7 *0.01*

The first surprise. Instead of

25

the customary Grünfeld Defence, which the two players persistently 'polished' in their previous matches, Kasparov employs the double-edged King's Indian Defence. Back in their first clash in 1984-85 many experts assumed that this opening, which was firmly established in the Black repertoire of Kasparov-the-Challenger, would be the chief topic of the theoretical argument between the two outstanding players. But only once – in the 17th game of the 1987 match – did Kasparov remember about the King's Indian Defence. And now, in the opening game of the fifth successive match between these long-standing opponents, Kasparov-the-Champion once again 'uncovers' this old but formidable weapon.

| 4 | e4 | *0.01* | d6 | *0.01* |
| 5 | f3 | *0.01* | | |

An answering surprise. Karpov

has only very rarely employed the Sämisch Variation. From the very first moves it is clear that both players are aiming for uncompromising play.

Initially the idea of 5 f3 was to prepare queenside castling followed by an attack on the kingside: g2-g4 and h2-h4-h5. The drawback to the variation is its slowness. When Eduard Gufeld, an inveterate King's Indian player, was asked what he thought about the move 5 f3, he wittily replied: "You would do better to ask the knight at g1!".

Black's play in the Sämisch Variation is based on undermining the white pawn centre by ... e5, ... c5 or ... b5. In the present game he defers ... e5 and mounts a pawn offensive on the queenside. At the same time, this demonstration of force is directed against White's possible queenside castling.

5	...		0-0	*0.06*
6	♗e3	*0.01*	c6	*0.06*
7	♗d3	*0.04*	a6	*0.09*

7 ... e5 8 d5 b5 has occurred in Kasparov's games, but the pawn sacrifice is not altogether correct. A recent example is Gulko-Kasparov (Linares 1990).

8	♘ge2	*0.06*	b5	*0.10*
9	0-0	*0.09*	♘bd7	*0.15*
10	♖c1	*0.16*		

This move is directed against the idea of 10 ... bxc4 11 ♗xc4

♘b6 12 ♗b3 a5: after 13 ♘a4 the black bishop cannot go to a6. Another possibility in this position is 10 a3. Taimanov-Geller (Moscow 1967) continued 10 ... bxc4 11 ♗xc4 a5 12 ♖c1 ♗a6 13 ♗xa6 ♖xa6 14 ♘a4 ♕a8 15 ♘ec3 ♖b8, and Black equalised.

10 cxb5 axb5 11 b4 comes into consideration. Geller-Fischer (Havana 1965) went 11 ... e5 12 ♕d2 exd4 13 ♘xd4 ♗b7 14 ♖fd1 ♘e5 15 ♗f1 ♘fd7 16 a4, with a slight advantage for White.

10	...		e5	*0.22*
11	a3	*0.36*		

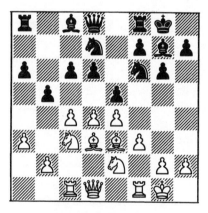

A new move, but, as we will soon see, an inaccurate one. Sooner or later White will have to take on b5, and he should have done this immediately, so as not to leave Black any choice: after 11 cxb5 it would be unsatisfactory to reply 11 ... cxb5 on account of 12 d5, when the position is blocked,

whereas Black would like to have some possibility of opening the game.

In Diez del Corral-Spassky (Palma de Mallorca 1969) 11 b3 was played, but after 11 ...exd4 12 ♘xd4 ♘e5 13 cxb5 axb5 14 ♗e2 d5 Black gained a slight advantage.

11	...		exd4	*0.45*
12	♘xd4	*0.36*	♗b7	*0.46*
13	cxb5	*0.50*	cxb5!	*0.55*

This is the whole point! Black activates his bishop on the long diagonal, and his isolated d-pawn can advance at the required moment.

14	♖e1	*1.20*	♘e5	*1.13*

Black has comfortably deployed his pieces and has already achieved a satisfactory game. It is no accident that Karpov thought for a long time over his previous move. An active plan for White would be to put pressure on the d-file, but at the moment this is hardly possible. Consequently the prophylactic plan chosen by the Ex-World Champion deserves approval. In anticipation of the opening of the position White withdraws his bishops from possible attacks and at the same time clears the central files for his heavy pieces.

15	♗f1	*1.22*	♖e8	*1.16*
16	♗f2	*1.30*	d5	*1.35*

This advance could have been delayed, since the move would not have run away. 16 ... ♖c8 was preferable. Perhaps Kasparov, satisfied with such a favourable solving of the problem of the black pieces in the first game, wanted immediately to clarify the position.

17   exd5   *1.32*   ♘xd5   *1.37*
18   ♘xd5   *1.44*

Some of the experts in the press centre recommended 18 ♘e4, but such play is not in Karpov's style. After 18 ... ♘f4 19 ♘c5 ♕g5 White would have faced dangerous threats, e.g. 20 g3 ♗d5 21 ♗e3 ♘ed3, or 21 ♘e4 ♗xe4 22 ♖xe4 ♘ed3.

**18 ...			♕xd5** *1.52*

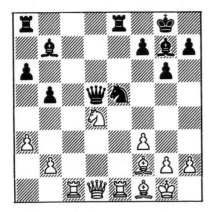

Black should have seriously considered capturing on d5 with his bishop, followed by bringing out his queen to f6 or g5 and ... ♖ad8. The attempt to prevent

this by 19 ♘b3 meets with a combinational refutation: 19 ... ♘xf3+ 20 gxf3 ♕g5+ and then 21 ... ♖xe1 22 ♕xe1 ♗xb3. After 19 ♘c2 a sacrifice on f3 is again possible, but this time of the bishop: 19 ... ♗xf3 20 ♕xd8 ♖axd8 21 gxf3 ♘xf3+ 22 ♔g2 ♘xe1+ 23 ♗xe1 ♗xb2, with advantage to Black. The simple 19 ... ♗c4 is also possible. Kasparov was perhaps afraid of 19 a4, but here too the simplest reply is 19 ... ♗c4 20 axb5 axb5 21 ♘xb5 ♗xf1 followed by ... ♘d3.

19   a4!   *1.50*

White cannot delay! If Black succeeds in placing his queen's rook at d8 he will gain a clear advantage. Here one notices a characteristic feature: in the first games of a match Karpov begins playing actively only when his opponent forces him to.

**19 ...			♗h6?** *1.52*

Quickly played, but an inexplicable decision. Black's idea was evidently revealed in other variations (e.g. *20 ♖c7 ♗f4*), but the World Champion simply 'forgot' that the rook could move back.

19 ... ♖ad8 would have led to interesting play, not unfavourable for Black, for example: 20 axb5 axb5 21 ♗xb5 ♘xf3+ (the tempting *21 ... ♘g4* does not work in

view of *22 ☐xe8+ ☐xe8 23 ♗xe8 ♘xf2 24 ♗xf7+! ♔xf7 25 ☐c7+ ♔f8 26 ♘e6+ ♕xe6 27 ♕d8+)* 22 ♕xf3 ☐xe1+ 23 ☐xe1 ♗xd4 with an equal game. And in the event of 21 ♘xb5 ♕e6 Black has active play, fully compensating for the pawn: 22 ♕c2 ♕f6 23 ♗g3 ♗h6 24 ☐cd1 *(24 ♗xe5 ☐xe5 25 ☐xe5 ♕xe5* does not get White out of his difficulties; Black has a strong attack on the dark squares) 24 ... ♘xf3+ 25 gxf3 ♕xf3 26 ♗g2 ♗e3+ 27 ♔h1 ☐xd1 28 ☐xd1 ♗f2! and wins. Therefore in this variation White must continue 23 ♘d4 ☐xd4 24 ♗xd4 ♘xf3+ 25 gxf3 ♕g5+ 26 ♗g2 *(26 ♕g2* is bad on account of *26 ... ♗xd4+ 27 ♔h1 ☐xe1 28 ☐xe1 ♗xf3)* 26 ... ♗xd4+ 27 ♔h1 ♗e5 28 ♕f2 ♕f4 29 ♕g3 ♕xc1 30 ☐xc1 ♗xg3 31 hxg3 ☐e3 32 ☐c3 ☐e1+ 33 ♔h2 ☐e2, when Black has everything in order.

19 ... ☐ed8 was also quite good.

20 ☐a1! *1.50* ♘c4 *2.09*

This leads to the loss of a pawn. It was essential to play 20 ... b4.

21 axb5 *1.53* axb5 *2.10*

(see diagram)

22 ☐xa8? *1.58*

The obvious move, but a mistake. The exchange on e8 was more accurate, when White would have remained a pawn up without

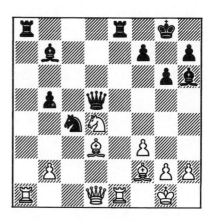

Black having any counterplay: 22 ☐xe8+ ☐xe8 23 ♘xb5 ♕xd1 24 ☐xd1 ♘xb2 25 ☐b1 ♗g7 26 ♗d4 ♘a4 27 ♗xg7 ♔xg7 28 ♘d6!. The point is that the rook at e8 is the victim of a knight fork! 23 ... ♘xb2 also does not help, the simplest being 24 ♕xd5 ♗xd5 25 ♘c7 ☐d8 26 ♗d4 ♗g7 27 ♗xb2 ♗xb2 28 ☐d1, winning a piece, while after 23 ... ♕xb5 24 b3 ♗d5 25 ☐a4 White emerges a pawn up.

The following day it became known that 'Deep Thought', the world-famous IBM chess computer, had analysed this position and given its verdict: by 22 b3 White could have won a pawn. This analysis was reported to the Karpov team, and after some time came the reply that the computer was right. Two replies were considered:

(a) 22 ... ☐xe1 23 ☐xa8+ ♗xa8 24 ♕xe1 ♘d2 *(24 ... ♘d6 25 ♘xb5!*

♘xb5 26 ♕e8+ and 27 ♕xb5) 25 ♗xb5 ♘xb3 26 ♕e8+, and now 26 ... ♗f8 27 ♘xb3 ♕xb3 28 ♗c5 and mates, or 26 ... ♔g7 27 ♘xb3 ♕xb3 28 ♗d4+ f6 29 ♕e7+ ♔g8 30 ♕d8+ ♗f8 31 ♗c5 ♕f7 32 ♗c4, also leading to mate.

(b) 22 ... ♘d6 23 ♖xe8+ ♖xe8 24 ♘xb5! ♘xb5 25 ♕xd5 ♗xd5 26 ♗xb5, and White is a healthy pawn to the good.

To all appearances, this analysis is correct, but after the possible reply 22 ... ♘d2, not considered by the computer, a tense position arises (*23 ♖xa8 ♖xa8 24 ♗xb5 ♗f4*) where Black has sufficient compensation for the pawn; it is difficult for White to find a move, and Black can strengthen his position by ... h5 etc.

22	...	♖xa8	*2.10*
23	♕b3	*2.03*	

23 ♘xb5 did not achieve anything, in view of 23 ... ♕xd1 24 ♖xd1 ♘xb2 25 ♖b1 ♗g7 26 ♗d4 ♘a4, but not 23 ... ♘xb2 24 ♕b1, or 23 ... ♕xb5 24 b3 ♗d5 25 ♖e5!.

23	...	♗c6	*2.12*
24	♗d3	*2.06*	

Black also maintains the balance after 24 ♘xc6 ♕xc6 25 ♕c2 ♖c8 (the more active *25 ... ♖d8* is also possible).

24	...	♘d6!	*2.13*

A temporary pawn sacrifice. Kasparov has accurately calculated that within a few moves he can restore material equality.

25	♕xd5	*2.08*	♗xd5	*2.13*
26	♘xb5	*2.09*	♘xb5	*2.13*
27	♗xb5	*2.09*	♗g7	*2.14*
28	b4	*2.14*	♗c3	*2.15*
29	♖d1	*2.14*	♗b3	*2.15*
30	♖b1	*2.23*		

No better is 30 ♖c1 ♗d2! 31 ♖b1 ♗c2 32 ♖b2? ♖a1+ 33 ♗f1 ♗d3.

30	...	♗a2	*2.15*

The white rook is tied to the first rank, and so it cannot escape from the pursuit of the bishops.

Draw agreed

GAME TWO   10 October

A slight surprise – Kasparov began the game by moving his king's pawn, which in his meetings with Karpov has not occurred very often. The last time that he played this was in the 1986 match in London/ Leningrad. As was the case four years ago, in reply Karpov employed his main weapon with Black – the Ruy Lopez.

For his boldness one has to give the Ex-World Champion his due: he chose a variation in which he had suffered two painful defeats at the hands of Kasparov – in Games 14 and 16 from the 1986 match. Perhaps he was encouraged by the game Ivanchuk-Karpov, Linares 1989 (up to move 18 the two games were identical), in which Black gained a draw without difficulty. But with his next two moves Kasparov employed a new plan and set Black some difficult problems.

White gained a great positional advantage, and it was not surprising that he was able to find a clear-cut combinational solution – the sacrifice of two pieces for a rook. True, many experts thought this sacrifice to be a mistake – the white knight which penetrated onto the 8th rank was lost by force. But the World Champion's idea soon became clear: a position was reached where the black pieces lacked coordination, whereas the white rooks, usually unwieldy, were active and manoeuvrable. Karpov spent a great deal of time in thought, but failed to find a satisfactory defence. When Black's time trouble ended he was the exchange down with an inferior position. The match arbiter had already prepared the sealed move envelope when Karpov congratulated the opponent on his win.

And so, after his very first 'White' game the World Champion had taken the lead in the match.

As Kasparov admitted after the game, the theoretical innovation which brought him success had been awaiting its hour since 1984.

	Kasparov-Karpov				2	♘f3	*0.01*	♘c6	*0.02*
	Ruy Lopez				3	♗b5	*0.01*	a6	*0.02*
					4	♗a4	*0.01*	♘f6	*0.02*
1	e4	*0.01*	e5	*0.02*	5	0-0	*0.01*	♗e7	*0.02*

31

6	♖e1	0.02	b5	0.02
7	♗b3	0.02	d6	0.02
8	c3	0.02	0-0	0.02
9	h3	0.02	♗b7	0.04
10	d4	0.02	♖e8	0.04

Thus begins the variation devised by Karpov's constant trainer, Grandmaster Igor Zaitsev, a variation which just as constantly and faithfully serves the Ex-World-Champion when playing Black against 1 e4.

The idea of this variation is to accelerate the pressure on e4, without wasting time on ... h6 (as in the Smyslov Variation), and thereby prevent the customary 'Spanish' manoeuvre of the queen's knight: ♘b1-d2-f1-g3.

11　♘bd2　0.02

Experience has shown that White cannot immediately exploit the weakening of f7. For example, 11 ♘g5 ♖f8 12 f4 exf4 13 ♗xf4 ♘a5 14 ♗c2 ♘d5, with a roughly equal game.

11	...		♗f8	0.05
12	a4	0.04		

It is clear that 12 ♘f1 is not possible on account of the loss of ethe e4 pawn, and so White must find another plan. 12 ♘g5 again does not achieve anything, in view of 12 ... ♖e7 13 f4 h6 14 ♘df3 ♕e8! 15 fxe5 dxe5 16 dxe5 ♖d8!, with advantage to Black (Arnason-Geller, Reykjavik 1986).

12 ♗c2 is also played, with the idea of shutting Black's light-square bishop out of the game by d4-d5, b2-b3 and c3-c4. 12 a3 has also occurred, as, for example, in one of the games from the Timman-Portisch match, Antwerp 1989, where 12 ... h6 13 ♗c2 ♘b8 14 b4 ♘bd7 15 ♗b2 g6 16 ♖b1 ♖b8 led to a complicated manoeuvring game with roughly equal chances.

12　...　　　　h6　0.06

The 46th game of the terminated Kasparov-Karpov match (Moscow 1984-85) went 12 ... ♕d7 13 axb5 axb5 14 ♖xa8 ♗xa8 15 d5, and after 15 ... ♘d8? 16 ♘f1 h6 17 ♘3h2 ♘b7 18 ♗c2 ♘c5 19 b4 ♘a6 20 ♘g4 White gained an obvious advantage.

But in the 5th game of their next match (Moscow 1985) Karpov improved with 15 ... ♘a5, and Black obtained a fully equal game.

13	♗c2	0.05	exd4	0.08
14	cxd4	0.05	♘b4	0.08
15	♗b1	0.05	bxa4	0.10

One of the key positions in the Zaitsev Variation. Black's pressure on e4 hinders the regrouping of the white pieces, and White must reinforce his centre in order to develop his queenside forces. The alternative plan is to immediately attack the white centre with 15 ... c5.

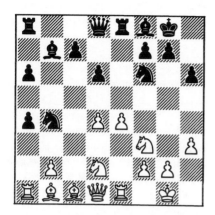

| 16 | ℤxa4 | *0.06* | a5 | *0.10* |
| 17 | ℤa3 | *0.06* | | |

The rook comes into play along the third rank, with the possibility of moving to e3 or g3.

| 17 | ... | | ℤa6 | *0.11* |

An analogous manoeuvre. This seemingly strange move has the idea of including the rook in the defence of the kingside.

| 18 | ♘h2 | *0.13* | | |

This is how events developed in the game A.Sokolov-Geller, Riga 1985, after 18 ℤae3: 18 ... a4 19 ♘f1 d5 20 e5 ♘e4 21 ♘1d2 c5 23 ♘xe4 dxe4 24 ♗xe4 ♗xe4 25 ℤxe4 c4, and White does not have e5-e6. Black is a pawn down, but the light-square blockade gives him a fully equal game.

In the first game of the Timman-Karpov Final Candidates Match, Kuala Lumpur 1990, the Dutch grandmaster's 18 ♘h4 met with a refutation: 18 ... ♘xe4 19 ♘xe4 ♗xe4 20 ♗xe4 d5! 21 ℤae3 ℤae6 (*21 ... dxe4!? 22 ℤxe4 ℤxe4 23 ℤxe4 ♕d5!*) 22 ♗g6!? ♕xh4 23 ℤxe6 ℤxe6 24 ℤxe6 fxe6 25 ♗e3 ♕f6.

| 18 | ... | | g6 | *0.11* |
| 19 | f3! | *0.15* | | |

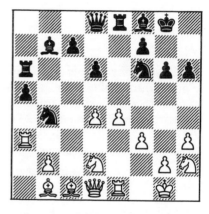

An important theoretical innovation. Kasparov rejects the standard continuations and reinforces his centre, in order to complete the mobilisation of his queenside. Now Black does not have any active play. He is forced to switch to defence and to conduct it with exceptional accuracy.

Here is how this position was handled by Ivanchuk in his meeting with Karpov at Linares 1989: 19 f4 d5 20 e5 ♘e4 21 ♘g4 c5 22 ♘xe4 dxe4 23 dxc5 ♗xc5+ 24 ♗e3 ♗f8 25 ♘f6+ ℤxf6 26 ♕xd8 ℤxd8 27 exf6 ♘d3 28 ℤd1 ♗xa3

29 bxa3 ♗d5, and the players agreed a draw.

19 ...   ♛d7   0.21

The first inaccuracy. The knight should have been prevented from going to c4, where it will occupy a strong position in the centre. This would have been achieved by 19 ... ♗a8, when 20 ♘c4 can be met by 20 ... d5.

20   ♘c4!   0.36   ♛b5   0.24
21   ♖c3   0.38   ♗c8   0.34

Here Karpov should have tried to gain counterplay with 21 ... d5, leading to a very sharp position. Even so, after 22 ♘a3 ♛b6 23 e5 ♘d7 24 f4 c5 25 ♗e3 White's threats are very dangerous.

22   ♗e3   0.44   ♔h7   1.03
23   ♛c1   0.59

23 ♛d2 was also possible, leaving c1 free for the doubling of rooks. But Kasparov assigns another role to his king's rook, since he has in mind a plan of attacking along the h-file (♘*h2-g4*).

23   ...   c6?   1.06

A serious tactical mistake. This not only weakens d6, but more important – the rook at a6 is cut off from the defence of the kingside. 23 ... ♛b8 was preferable (with the threat of ... *d5*), for example 24 ♘a3 c6 25 ♘g4 ♘g8, with only a slight advantage to

White, since his knight at a3 is out of play and cannot return to c4 on account of ... d5.

24   ♘g4   1.18   ♘g8   1.26

Black's final mistake. It was essential to play 24 ... ♗xg4 25 hxg4 ♛b8, with the hope of meeting White's attack on the h-file by countering in the centre. For example, 26 ♔f2 d5 27 ♗xh6 ♗xh6 28 ♖h1 ♘g8 29 ♘e5 ♖xe5 (or *29 ... ♛a7*) 30 dxe5 ♛xe5, and Black parries the attack.

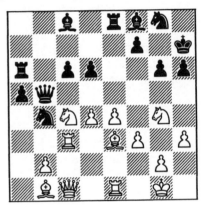

25   ♗xh6!! *1.34*

An unexpected blow. Many experts thought that the World Champion had made an oversight in this combination, since the white knight at e8 proves to be trapped. However, the difficulty lay not in the calculation but in the evaluation of the resulting position. As soon becomes clear, Kasparov has foreseen all the consequences of his combination.

25	...		♗xh6	*1.28*
26	♘xh6	*1.35*	♘xh6	*1.28*
27	♘xd6	*1.35*	♕b6	*1.28*
28	♘xe8	*1.39*		

Here Karpov thought for a long time. Evidently he now realised that his position was very difficult. Perhaps he also considered the immediate 28 ... ♕d8, which would probably have delayed the attack, but White's positional advantage would have left Black with no hope of saving the game.

28	...		♕xd4+	*1.50*
29	♔h1	*1.40*	♕d8	*1.50*
30	♖d1	*1.48*	♕xe8	*1.50*
31	♕g5	*1.48*		

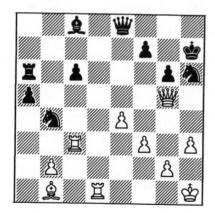

Here is the position obtained by force as a result of White's seven-move combination. White has a superiority in attacking force and his pieces are splendidly co-ordinated, whereas Black's pieces are scattered and his knight at b4 is altogether out of play.

31	...		♖a7	*1.58*

31 ... ♘g8, with the idea of meeting 32 ♖d8 with 32 ... ♕e7, fails to the intermediate check 32 ♕h4+, when 32 ... ♔g7 33 ♖d8 ♕e6 34 f4 leads to an overwhelming position for White.

32	♖d8	*1.51*	♕e6	*1.58*
33	f4	*1.54*	♗a6	*2.11*

No better is 33 ... ♖d7 34 f5 ♕d6 (*34 ... ♖xd8 35 fxe6 ♖d1+ 36 ♔h2 ♖xb1 37 e7*) 35 ♖xc8 ♕d1+ 36 ♔h2 ♕xb1 37 ♖h8+ ♔xh8 38 ♕xh6+ ♔g8 39 f6, with inevitable mate.

34	f5	*1.57*	♕e7	*2.21*
35	♕d2	*2.01*		

After 35 ♖h8+ ♔xh8 36 ♕xh6+ ♔g8 37 fxg6 f6 the outcome is not at all clear. Kasparov's temporary retreat is the most certain way to win.

35	...		♕e5	*2.26*

35 ... ♘d5 fails to 36 ♖h8+.

36	♕f2	*2.04*	♕e7	*2.28*
37	♕d4	*2.05*	♘g8	*2.28*
38	e5	*2.06*	♘d5	*2.29*
39	fxg6+	*2.18*	fxg6	*2.29*
40	♖xc6	*2.20*	♕xd8	*2.29*
41	♕xa7+	*2.21*	♘de7	*2.29*
42	♖xa6	*2.22*	♕d1+	*2.30*
43	♕g1	*2.22*	♕d2	*2.30*
44	♕f1	*2.23*	**Resigns**	

GAME THREE

15/16 October

The third game was played after a break, since on the previous match day Karpov had taken one of the three postponements allowed by the regulations to each player during the entire match. A responsible decision! After all only two of the 24 games had been played! But the poor start to the match evidently demanded serious reflection and, perhaps, changes to his match strategy. It is also possible that a study of some concrete opening variations was required.

Again, as in Game 1, Kasparov chose the King's Indian Defence, and it can be assumed that, for the present match, he has chosen this opening as one of his main defensive weapons as Black. Karpov, dissatisfied with the outcome of the opening stage of the first game, on this occasion avoided the Sämisch Variation.

On move 9 Kasparov employed an innovation (confirmation that the King's Indian had been thoroughly prepared), inviting the opponent to win the exchange for a pawn. But the sacrificing did not end at that! After Karpov had missed a favourable opportunity (13 ♕d3!), with his 14th move the World Champion offered a positional sacrifice of queen for only two minor pieces! Karpov did not immediately accept this generous gift, and when he did so, it turned out that White faced a difficult defence. The black pieces, splendidly coordinated, dominated the centre, while White's pieces were pushed back, and his strongest piece simply could not find suitable employment. In the end Karpov relieved the situation by giving back his queen. The balance of the forces became more commonplace: Black had two pawns for the exchange and a marked advantage. Not long before the break Kasparov played inaccurately, and the white pieces acquired long-awaited activity. After the adjournment the play was more or less forced, and a mass elimination of material took this fantastic game to a peaceful end.

				2	c4	0.00	g6	0.00
Karpov-Kasparov				3	♘c3	0.00	♗g7	0.01
King's Indian Defence				4	e4	0.00	d6	0.01
1	d4	0.00	♘f6	0.00	5	♘f3	0.01	0-0	0.01

36

6 ♗e2 *0.01* **e5** *0.02*
7 ♗e3 *0.02*

The Gligorić Variation. By deferring kingside castling for the moment, White to a certain extent neutralises Black's counterplay involving a kingside pawn offensive after 7 0-0 ♘c6 8 d5 ♘e7 (if *7 ♗e3 ♘c6 8 d5 ♘e7 9 ♘d2* Black's offensive loses its main object of attack – the white king).

White also avoids the simplifying variation 7 0-0 ♘c6 8 ♗e3 ♖e8 9 d5 ♘d4, with equality.

7 ... **♕e7** *0.06*

In view of the threat of 8 ... exd4 9 ♘xd4 ♘xe4 White has to determine the position in the centre. Another way of exploiting White's last move is by 7 ... ♘g4.

8 dxe5 *0.07* **dxe5** *0.07*
9 ♘d5 *0.07* **♕d8?!** *0.07*

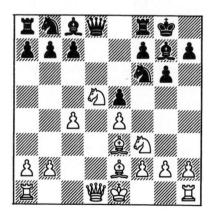

The first time this has occurred

in a serious game. Although the play developed favourably for Black, thanks to the effect of surprise, it is unlikely that this idea will be repeated, and that includes by the inventor himself.

The usual continuation in this position is 9 ... ♘xd5 10 cxd5 ♖d8 11 0-0 ♘d7 12 ♕c2 ♘f6 13 ♗g5 h6 14 ♗xf6 ♗xf6 15 ♖ac1, with a minimal advantage to White in Portisch-Geller, Portorož 1973.

10 ♗c5 *0.21*

It turns out that this position had already been reached in a game Peek-Canfell, Dieren 1988, where after 10 ... ♖e8?? 11 ♗e7! Black resigned.

10 ... **♘xe4** *0.07*

Black sacrifices the exchange for a pawn, and gives the play an unusual character.

11 ♗e7! *0.30*

Before winning the exchange, White forces the black queen to an unfavourable square.

11 ... **♕d7** *0.08*
12 ♗xf8 *0.32* **♔xf8** *0.09*
13 ♕c2? *0.36*

A mistake, after which Black's idea proves justified. It is clear that, if the position is consolidated, Black will have more than sufficient compensation for the sacrificed material: a strong King's Indian bishop and a pawn centre.

The white queen is unpromisingly placed at c2; moreover, here it comes under attack by the minor pieces. The only way to cast doubt on Black's idea was by active play, and this could have been achieved with 13 ♕d3!, e.g. 13 ... ♘d6 (best) 14 ♕a3 ♘c6 (*14 ... c6 15 ♘b6*) 15 ♖d1.

13	**...**	♘c5	*0.15*
14	**♖d1**	*0.40*	♘c6!	*0.21*

In various lines Black is ready to give up his queen for two minor pieces. For example, 15 ♘b6 axb6 16 ♖xd7 ♗xd7.

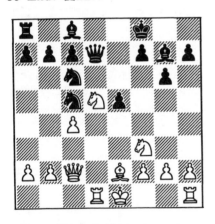

15	**0-0**	*1.10*

This was perhaps the last point when Karpov could have fought for the initiative – 15 ♘g5 ♕d8 16 ♘f6 ♘d4 17 ♘gxh7+ ♔e7 18 ♖xd4 exd4 19 ♘d5+ ♔e8, or 15 ... ♔g8 16 ♘f6+ ♗xf6 17 ♖xd7 ♗xd7 18 ♘e4 ♘xe4 19 ♕xe4,

with a double-edged game.

15	**...**	♘e6	*1.02*

Black is ready to place a knight at d4 and fully consolidate the position, as mentioned above. This factor evidently persuades Karpov to accept the queen sacrifice.

16	**♘b6?**	*1.30*

Even so, White should have rejected the Greek gift – the resulting position is too cheerless for him. In our opinion, 16 ♖fe1 ♘cd4 17 ♘xd4 ♘xd4 18 ♕c3 was preferable.

16	**...**	axb6	*1.02*
17	**♖xd7**	*1.30*	♗xd7	*1.02*

White has a material advantage, but the four black minor pieces coordinate splendidly, both in defence and in attack. In addition, with a pawn offensive Black can drive back the white pieces onto the first rank. It is also not clear how to solve the problem of the a2 pawn, which is under attack. It is evident that Black has a threatening initiative and that White faces a difficult defence.

18	**♕d2?!**	*1.37*

Good drawing chances were offered by 18 ♖d1 ♘ed4 19 ♘xd4 ♘xd4 20 ♖xd4 exd4.

18	**...**	♗e8	*1.07*
19	**b3**	*1.41*	e4	*1.16*
20	**♘e1**	*1.43*	f5	*1.38*

21 &d1   *1.49*

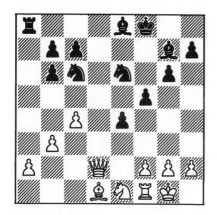

21 ...   De5   *1.47*

21 ... &f7 would perhaps be better, bringing up another piece.

22 Dc2   *1.54*

White sacrifices a pawn, in an attempt to activate his pieces.

22 ...   Exa2   *1.51*
23 Wd5   *1.56*   **&e7**   *1.52*

The alternative here was 23 ... Ea5, when after both 24 Wxb7 &c6 25 Wc8+ &f7, and 24 Wxe6 &d7 the queen is trapped. But after 24 Wd2 Ea8 25 f3 White obtains active play.

24 Db4   *2.02*   **c6**   *2.07*

24 ... &c6 was probably more accurate. Then after 25 Wxc6 bxc6 26 Dxa2 &h6! (with the threat of 27... &d2, shutting the white knight out of the game) the opposite-colour bishops favour the attack-

ing side. Slightly better is 25 Wxe6+ &xe6 26 Dxa2 b5, when Black undoubles his pawns.

25 Wxe6+ *2.02*   **&xe6**   *2.07*
26 Dxa2   *2.03*

As a result of the entire operation, Black has two pawns for the exchange and strongly placed minor pieces, but the realisation of his advantage is made difficult by his doubled pawns on the queenside. In the near future the undoubling of these pawns is one of Black's main problems.

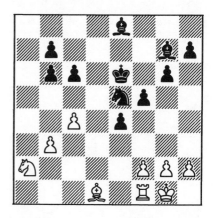

26 ...   Df7   *2.09*

Black manoeuvres his knight to d6, where it will occupy an ideal position, fulfilling both attacking and defensive duties.

27 &e2   *2.08*   **Dd6**   *2.11*
28 Db4   *2.10*   **&c3**   *2.14*

28 ... b5 29 cxb5 c5 was an interesting possibility, but Kasparov

prefers first to restrict White by strengthening his position in the centre and on the kingside.

29	♘c2	2.10	f4	2.14
30	♖d1	2.14	h5	2.18
31	f3	2.15		

There is no future in marking time. Although White allows Black a protected passed pawn, he gains the d3 square for his bishop.

31	...		e3	2.19
32	g3	2.17	g5	2.19
33	♗d3	2.17		

The attempt to break up Black's pawn phalanx by 33 h4 fails to 33 ... ♘f5.

| 33 | ... | | h4 | 2.21 |

Now h2-h4 was a threat.

| 34 | ♔f1 | 2.20 | | |

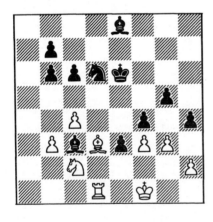

| 34 | ... | | c5 | 2.21 |

Black begins playing actively on the queenside. Possibly Kasparov wanted to suppress White's counterplay on the g-file, e.g. 35 gxf4 gxf4 36 ♔e2 and 37 ♖g1, but in our opinion this plan did not hold any great dangers for Black. He could have first regrouped his forces and then carried out his plan in a more favourable situation: 34 ... ♗e5 35 ♔e2 ♔f6. Now in the event of 36 gxh4 gxh4 37 ♖g1 ♗h5 38 ♖g8 Black has 38 ... ♘f7, with the terrible threat of ... ♘g5. With the c6 pawn at c5 this plan is ineffective, since White has ♗e4.

35	♔e2	2.22	b5	2.26
36	cxb5	2.25	♘xb5	2.26
37	♗c4+	2.25	♔e7	2.26

Many commentators criticised Kasparov for this move, and suggested 37 ... ♔f6 instead. Let us examine this continuation: 38 ♖d8 ♘c7 39 gxf4 gxf4 40 ♖c8 ♗e5 41 ♘e1 b5 42 ♗g8 ♔g7 (♗g6) 43 ♘d3 ♗d6 44 ♖d8 and the black pieces are thrown back. Kasparov prefers to give up a pawn but retain the initiative.

| 38 | ♖d5 | 2.26 | ♗f6 | 2.27 |
| 39 | ♖xc5 | 2.27 | | |

No better was 39 gxf4 ♘c3+ 40 ♔xe3 ♘xd5+ 41 ♗xd5 b5, when White maintains material equality, but Black has an undisputed positional advantage.

| 39 | ... | | ♘c3+ | 2.28 |
| 40 | ♔f1 | 2.29 | ♗g6 | 2.29 |

41 ♘e1 *2.29*

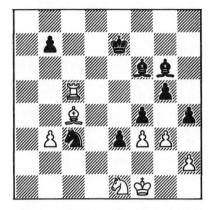

In this position Kasparov sealed his 41st move.

The initial assessment of many grandmasters was as follows: the position favours White, but the most probable outcome is a draw. But analysis showed that the protected passed pawn and the activity of the black minor pieces fully compensated for White's material advantage, and it was then Kasparov's chances which were thought to be better.

41 ... **♚d6** *2.38*

Many experts considered 41 ... b6 to be stronger, but in this case White has sufficient defensive resources, e.g. 42 ♖c6 b5 43 ♗d3 ♗xd3 (*43 ... ♗e8 44 ♖a6*) 44 ♘xd3 hxg3 45 hxg3 fxg3 46 ♚g2 ♘e2 47 ♘e1.

42 ♖a5! *2.29*

42 ♖c8 was significantly worse

on account of 42 ... ♗f5 43 ♖f8 ♗h3+ 44 ♚g1 ♗d4 45 gxf4 e2+ 46 ♚h1 gxf4! (of course, not *46 ... ♗f2? 47 fxg5 ♗xe1 48 g6*). Now after 47 ♖f4 ♗f2, 47 ♖e8 ♗e3 or 47 ♖d8+ ♗d7 White in all cases loses a piece.

42	...		**fxg3**	*2.38*
43	**hxg3**	*2.31*	**hxg3**	*2.38*
44	**♘g2**	*2.31*	**b5**	*2.39*
45	**♖a6+**	*2.32*	**♚e7**	*2.39*
46	**♖a7+**	*2.42*	**♚e8**	*2.39*

Black achieves nothing by 46 ... ♚d8 47 ♗e2 ♗f5 (*47 ... ♗d4 48 ♖a6*) 48 ♖f7 ♘d5 49 ♚g1 ♗h3 50 ♖xf6 ♘xf6 51 ♘xe3, with a draw.

47 ♖a8+ *2.45* **♗d8** *2.39*

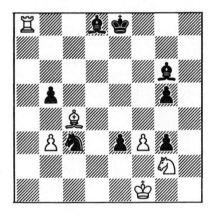

48	**♘xe3!**	*3.05*	**bxc4**	*2.41*
49	**♘xc4**	*3.05*	**g4**	*2.53*
50	**♚g2**	*3.11*	**♘e2**	*2.58*
51	**♘e5**	*3.15*	**gxf3+**	*2.58*
52	**♚xf3**	*3.16*	**g2**	*2.58*
53	**♖xd8+**	*3.16*		

Draw agreed

GAME FOUR   17 October

Today the flags disappeared from the chess table: the tri-coloured
Russian one, under which Kasparov was appearing, and the red flag
of Karpov. But it would seem that the 'flag war' was of most concern to
the officials in the Karpov team. The players themselves were more
interested in the outcome of the battle on the 64 black and white squares.

After the stormy and nervy 3rd game, which had lasted two days, it was
hard to expect an 'encore', but both players found both the desire and the
strength to conduct an even more gripping and complicated encounter.

Despite his defeat in the 2nd game, Karpov again played the Zaitsev
Variation. The sharp continuation chosen by him was designed to show
everyone, especially his opponent, that nothing terrible had happened,
and that the Ex-World Champion was capable of 'taking a blow'.
Kasparov happily accepted the challenge and, of course, gave as good as
he got: he threw onto the fire no more and no less than all of his queenside
pawns. His boats were burned; the World Champion was interested only
in the enemy king. But although in the resulting situation every tempo
was 'more precious than gold', Kasparov had sufficient composure and
imagination to make quiet moves such as 27 g3!. The veteran grandmaster
Miguel Najdorf, who has seen much throughout the present century,
excitedly tried to convince his colleagues in the press centre that no other
player in the world could have made such an unexpected move
(irrespective of its strength).

Yes, in this game there was much that was unexpected. About one
thing only did no one have any doubt: "There will be no draw today!"
And yet they were mistaken.

First Kasparov went wrong, missing the strongest continuation of the
attack, and then Karpov, just before the control, played a 'cooperative'
move, which allowed his opponent to force perpetual check.

	Kasparov-Karpov				2	♘f3	*0.03*	♘c6	*0.00*
	Ruy Lopez				3	♗b5	*0.03*	a6	*0.00*
					4	♗a4	*0.03*	♘f6	*0.01*
1	e4	*0.03*	e5	*0.00*	5	0-0	*0.04*	♗e7	*0.01*

6	♖e1	*0.04*	b5	*0.01*
7	♗b3	*0.04*	d6	*0.01*
8	c3	*0.04*	0-0	*0.01*
9	h3	*0.04*	♗b7	*0.02*

Once again the Zaitsev Variation.

10	d4	*0.04*	♖e8	*0.02*
11	♘bd2	*0.04*	♗f8	*0.02*
12	a4	*0.05*	h6	*0.06*
13	♗c2	*0.05*	exd4	*0.07*
14	cxd4	*0.05*	♘b4	*0.07*
15	♗b1	*0.06*	c5	*0.07*

After suffering a disaster in the 2nd game with 15 ... bxa4, Karpov chooses a continuation which he had already employed twice against Kasparov in their 1986 match.

16	d5	*0.06*		

White closes the centre, restricting the bishop at b7, after which he turns his attention to the kingside.

16	...		♘d7	*0.08*
17	♖a3	*0.07*		

The usual continuation here is 17 ♘f1, but then Black replies 17 ... f5, and the knight move proves to be a waste of time.

17	...		f5	*0.09*

It is surprising that such a risky continuation should continue to be practised. Black's kingside is permanently weakened, and this strategic factor will significantly influence the entire character of the play. It is even more surprising that such a sharp line should be played – not for the first time – by Karpov. Thus it occurred in Game 9 of the Final Candidates Match Timman-Karpov (Kuala Lumpur 1990), which went 18 ♖ae3 f4.

In Games 14 and 16 from the 1986 match Karpov played 17 ... c4, with the aim of gaining an outpost for his knight at d3.

18	exf5	*0.15*	♘f6	*0.10*
19	♘e4	*0.15*	♗xd5	*1.03*

It seems very surprising that Karpov should think for nearly an hour over a position which he must have analysed beforehand. In de Firmian-A.Ivanov, Las Vegas 1989, Black played 19 ... ♘bxd5, and the game continued 20 ♘h2 ♘xe4 21 ♗xe4 ♖xe4 22 ♖xe4 ♘c3 23 ♖xc3 ♗xe4 24 ♖g3 ♔h8 25 ♕g4 ♗d5 26 ♗d2?. Here, in his notes to the game (*Informator* 48), Ivanov recommends 26 b4!? ♕f6 27 ♗d2 cxb4 (*27 ... ♕a1+? 28 ♘f1 ♗c4 29 ♗c3 ♕xf1+ 30 ♔h2, with a won game*) 28 ♗b4 ♖c8 (if *28 ... ♕a1+ 29 ♘f1, with the idea on 29 ... ♖c8 of playing 30 f6*) 29 ♕d1!? ♕xf5 30 ♘g4, with compensation for the sacrificed material. This analysis is interesting, but unconvincing. Did Karpov know of it? At any event he chooses a different continuation.

20	♘xf6+	*0.39*	♕xf6	*1.04*

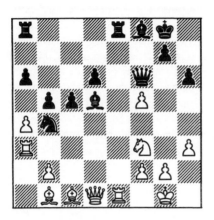

21   ♗d2?!   *0.51*

This move was recommended in the aforementioned analysis by Ivanov. It would be interesting to know whether Kasparov was familiar with it.

We consider that the idea carried out by Kasparov in this game is correct, but that it is incorrectly implemented. He should have first exchanged on b5: 21 axb5 axb5 (*21 ... ♖xe1+ 22 ♘xe1 axb5 23 ♘c2*, with a clear advantage to White) 22 ♗d2, obtaining the same attack as in the game, but without the great material sacrifices. Some sample variations: 22 ... ♖xa3 23 bxa3 ♖xe1+ 24 ♗xe1 ♗xf3 25 gxf3 ♘a6 26 a4, or 22 ... ♗xf3 23 ♖xf3, in each case with a clear advantage.

21   ...   **♛xb2**   *1.17*
22   ♗xb4   *0.57*   **♗f7!**   *1.22*

Retaining the important light-square bishop, which covers the chronic weaknesses in the black king's position.

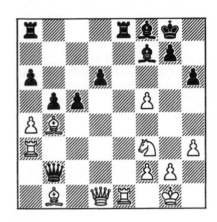

23   ♖e6!   *1.12*

The only resource to maintain any attacking chances for White. In the event of 23 axb5 ♛xb4 24 ♖xa6 ♖xe1+ 25 ♘xe1 (*25 ♛xe1 ♛xe1+ 26 ♘xe1 ♖b8*) 25 ... ♖e8 Black has the advantage (especially in the endgame).

23   ...   **♛xb4**   *1.30*

Both here and later we will see that ... ♗xe6, opening the diagonal for the white bishop, is dangerous for Black. In the given instance White has a strong attack after 23 ... ♗xe6 24 fxe6 cxb4 25 ♖b3 ♛f6 26 ♛d3 g6 (or *26 ... ♖xe6*) 27 ♖xb4.

24   ♖b3   *1.34*   **♛xa4**   *1.33*
25   ♗c2   *1.34*   **♖ad8!** *1.55*
26   ♖be3   *1.38*   **♛b4**   *1.56*

At the cost of two pawns, White has retained an attacking position. Now he must try and force Black to take on e6, thus opening the diagonal of the light-square bishop directly at the enemy king. It should be noted that Black's queen is shut off from his king by his own pawns, and this gives the attacking side additional possibilities.

27 g3! *1.49*

Kasparov vacates a good square for his king and simultaneously prepares to move his knight to h4. The direct 27 ♕e2 runs into 27 ... ♕c4 28 ♗d3 ♕c1+ 29 ♔h2 c4 30 ♗c2 ♗xe6.

27 g4 was tempting, with the threat of g4-g5. But evidently Kasparov instinctively sensed that the weakening of the f4 square could tell later, and so he avoided this continuation.

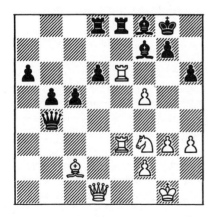

27 ... a5 *2.13*

The impression is that Black has no useful moves. True, the match bulletin gives a variation which was considered during the game by grandmasters Korchnoi and Christiansen: 27 ... d5 28 ♘e5 d4 29 ♖b3 ♗xe6! 30 ♖xb4 ♗xf5! 31 ♗xf5 ♖xe5, which would appear to be good for Black. But White too has a stronger continuation. To calculate at the board all the consequences of 27 ... d5 would hardly have been possible. The resulting position requires a detailed study. Probably Karpov did not want to weaken the e5 square, for where the white knight heads in various lines.

We give some possible continuations. 27 ... d5 28 ♖xe8 ♖xe8 29 ♖xe8 ♗xe8 30 ♕e2 ♗f7 (other bishop moves come to the same thing) 31 ♘e5 ♗e8 (*31 ... ♗e7 is bad on account of 32 ♘xf7 ♔xf7 33 ♕e6+ ♔e8 34 f6 gxf6 35 ♗g6+ ♔d8 36 ♗f5 ♔e8 37 ♕g8+ ♗f8 38 ♗g6+*, and White wins the bishop) 32 ♘c6 ♗xc6 33 ♕e6+ ♔h8 34 f6, with a mating attack. Had the white pawn been at g4 in this position (cf. the note to White's 27th move), then Black would have had the saving resource ... ♕f4!.

Therefore Black has no choice: he must attack the white pieces with 30 ... ♕c3 31 ♕xe8, and now:

(a) 31 ... ♕xf3 loses to 32 ♕e6+ ♔h7 33 f6+ ♔h8 34 fxg7+ ♗xg7 35 ♗f5! ♗d4 36 ♕xh6+ ♔g8 37

♗e6+ and mates, or 32 ... ♔h8 33 ♕f7 ♗d6 34 ♕e8+ ♔h7 35 f6+ and wins.

(b) 31 ... ♕xc2! 32 ♕e6+ ♔h7 (*32 ... ♔h8 33 ♘e5 ♕e4 34 ♘g6+ ♔h7 35 ♘xf8+ ♔h8 36 ♘g6+ ♔h7 37 ♕c8*) 33 ♕g6+ ♔g8 (*33 ... ♔h8 34 ♘e5 ♕d2 loses to 35 ♔g2!*, when against ♕f7 there is no defence) 34 ♘e5 ♕b1+ 35 ♔h2 ♕e1, and White must force a draw by 36 ♕f7+, since after 36 ♘g4 ♔h8! he might even lose.

28 ♘h4 *1.56*

The position is already ripe for decisive action: 28 ♕e2 ♕c4 29 ♗d3 ♗xe6 (*29 ... ♕d5 30 ♘h4* leads to lines examined below) 30 fxe6 (after *30 ♗xc4 ♗xc4* Black has more than sufficient compensation for the queen) 30 ... ♕d5 (*30 ... ♕c1+* shuts the queen out of the game: *31 ♔g2 c4 32 ♗f5 ♗e7 33 ♘d4 ♗f6 34 ♘c6*, or *31 ... ♗e7 32 ♗c2 ♗f6 33 ♕d3*, and there is no satisfactory defence against the threat of *35 ♕h7+ ♔f8 36 ♘h4*). Here White can force a draw by repetition: 31 ♗e4 ♕c4 32 ♗d3 ♕d5, which there is no sense in Black avoiding. He can also play for a win both with the 'mercenary' 33 ♗xb5 and by boldly continuing the attack – 33 ♘h4 ♗e7 34 ♗e4 ♕e5 (*34 ... ♕c4 35 ♕h5 ♗xh4 36 ♕f7+ ♔h8 37 ♕g6 ♔g8 38 ♕h7+ and wins*) 35 ♗b1 ♗xh4 36 ♖xe5 dxe5 37

gxh4 ♖xe6 38 ♕xb5 with advantage. 34 ♘g6! ♕xe6 35 ♗c2 is even stronger.

28 ... d5 *2.15*

Now White cannot wait any longer.

29	♕e2	*2.12*	♕c4	*2.15*
30	♗d3	*2.12*	♕c1+	*2.15*
31	♔g2	*2.12*	c4	*2.17*
32	♗c2	*2.13*	♗xe6	*2.25*

The alternative 32 ... d4, which looks very dangerous for White, would probably have led to a draw: 33 ♖xe8 ♖xe8 (*33 ... d3 is bad: 34 ♖xd8 dxe2 35 ♖xe2*, with mating threats after *♘g6*; also insufficient is *35 ... ♕g5 36 ♖b8 b4 37 ♘g6 ♗xg6 38 fxg6 b3 39 ♖ee8 ♕f6 40 ♗e4*, when White wins) 34 ♖xe8 d3 35 ♖xf8+ (but not *35 ♕e7 ♗xe8 36 ♕xe8 dxc2 37 ♘g6 ♕a3!*) 35 ... ♔xf8 36 ♕e5, and Black cannot avoid perpetual check.

33 ♖xe6? *2.19*

A mistake, after which White has to strive for a draw. He should play 33 fxe6, bringing the bishop into the attack. In this case it would be Black who would have to think in terms of saving the game: 33 ... ♗e7 34 ♘f5 ♕a1 35 ♕h5 ♕f6 36 ♖f3 ♕xe6 37 ♘d4 ♕d6 38 ♕f7+ ♔h8 39 ♘e6 ♗f6 40 ♕g6 ♔g8 41 ♖xf6, or 33 ... ♗c5 34 ♖f3 (not *34 ♗f5 ♗e3 35 ♕h5* on account of *35*

... ♕b2!, when White is obliged to give perpetual check) 34 ... ♖d6 35 ♗g6, with a powerful attack. The best defence for Black is 33 ... d4!. There can follow 34 ♗f5! ♖d5! 35 ♕h5 ♖xf5 36 ♕xf5 dxe2 37 ♕f7+ ♔h7 38 ♕g6+. This is perhaps the only line in which White is obliged to force perpetual check.

33	...	♖xe6	*2.26*
34	♕xe6+		*2.21*

White stubbornly refrains from opening the diagonal for his bishop. Here too it was correct to take with the pawn. For example, 34 fxe6 ♕g5 (*e6-e7* was threatened) 35 ♗g6 ♕f6 36 ♗f7+ ♔h7 37 ♕c2+ g6 38 ♘xg6 ♔g7 39 ♘f4, with a certain draw. Or 34 ... ♗e7 35 ♗g6 ♗xh4 36 gxh4 ♕f4 37 e7 ♕b8 (*37 ... ♕f6 38 e8=♕+ ♖xe8 39 ♕xe8+ ♕f8 40 ♗f7+*, or *38 ♕e6+*) 38 ♕e6+ ♔h8.

In this position Black has no satisfactory defence against the rapid advance of the white f-pawn: 39 f4! ♕c8 40 ♕f7 c3 41 f5 c2 42 f6 ♖g8 43 ♕xg8+! ♔xg8 44 f7+ ♔h8 45 f8=♕+! – Excelsior!*

34	...	♔h8	*2.26*
35	♘g6+	*2.22*	♔h7	*2.26*
36	♕e2	*2.22*	♕g5!	*2.27*

The attempt to remove the powerful X-ray threat of the bishop at c2 by 36 ... d4 37 f6 d3

would have led to a draw – 38 ♕e4 gxf6 39 ♘xf8++.

37	f6	*2.22*	♕xf6	*2.27*
38	♘xf8+	*2.23*	♔g8	*2.28*
39	♘g6	*2.23*		

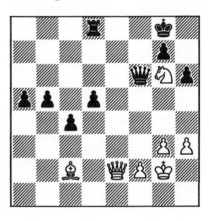

39	...	♕f7??	*2.28*

After obtaining a winning position, Karpov unexpectedly blocks an important square and allows White to force perpetual check. He could have won by 39 ... d4 40 ♗f5 ♕c6+ 41 ♗e4 (or *41 ♔g1 ♖e8 42 ♘e7+ ♔f8*) 41 ... d3! (but not *41 ... ♖e8? 42 ♗xc6 ♖xe2 43 ♗d5+ ♔h7 44 ♘f8+* with a draw) 42 ♘e7+ ♔f8 43 ♕f3+ ♕f6.

40	♘e7+	*2.24*	♔f8	*2.28*

Here the game was adjourned, but the following day, without resuming, the players agreed a **draw**.

---

* A name coined by the American problemist Sam Loyd for the composition task of advancing a pawn from the second to the eighth rank. (Translator's note)

GAME FIVE

22 October

After the 'mad' 4th game the World Champion took a postponement. Well, the strengths of even such experienced fighters as Kasparov and Karpov are not inexhaustible. Many chess observers commented that they could not recall another match for the World Championship that had started so fiercely.

However, in a long-distance race, an excessively frisky start can have unpleasant consequences at the finish. Therefore it came as no great surprise when the players conducted the 5th game in restrained positional style. Karpov was not ready to try and refute the World Champion's opening experiment in the King's Indian Defence (7 ... ♘a6), and Kasparov, in turn, was satisfied with accurate defence. The earlier disappearance of the queens, and then further mass exchanges, first of the rooks and then of several minor pieces, beat a certain path to a draw.

Of course, after the excitement of the start, both grandmasters needed a respite. But this was not the only factor that influenced the course of the game. There was one further reason, a purely psychological one, why Kasparov (and it is he who is usually the initiator of all sorts of complications in this match) should display caution on this occasion. The point is that, in his previous matches with Karpov, the 5th games had ended in a catastrophic score for the World Champion: +0 –3 =1. Need it be said that, for an impressionable grandmaster, and one who, like all players, believes in various signs, such a statistic exerts a very powerful psychological pressure.

Karpov-Kasparov
King's Indian Defence

1	d4	0.00	♘f6	0.00
2	c4	0.00	g6	0.00
3	♘c3	0.00	♗g7	0.00
4	e4	0.00	d6	0.01
5	♘f3	0.00	0-0	0.01
6	♗e2	0.01	e5	0.01

7 ♗e3   *0.01*   ♘a6?!   *0.01*

Kasparov, as we expected (see the commentary to Game 3), does not repeat the opening experiment which concluded successfully for him in that game. There could be no doubt that Karpov's team would have found an improvement.

48

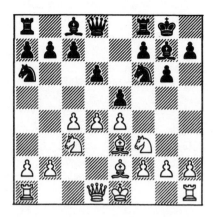

The move played is yet another experiment by the World Champion. At any event, it had not occurred previously in a serious game. Nor is it considered in Geller's theoretical monograph on the King's Indian Defence. The drawback to the move is obvious: the knight has gone to the edge of the board, but it could hardly be thought that the World Champion would not have taken this into account.

In the same book 7 ... c6 is recommended in the given position. In the event of 8 0-0 exd4 White must recapture with the bishop (*9 ♘xd4 ♖e8 10 f3 d5*), which is less active.

8 0-0 *0.11* **c6** *0.02*

Now the advantages of playing ... c6 a move earlier can be seen: Black would have had a wider choice of continuation.

9 dxe5 *0.31* **dxe5** *0.02*

After this exchange White can hardly count on a significant advantage. But maintaining the tension in the centre is also not easy. Perhaps 9 ♖e1 should have been seriously considered.

10 ♕xd8 *0.31* **♖xd8** *0.02*
11 ♖fd1 *0.31*

Nothing is achieved by 11 ♘xe5 ♘xe4 12 ♘xe4 ♗xe5 13 ♗g5, when both 13 ... ♖d4 and 13 ... ♖e8 ensure Black a good game.

11 ... **♖e8** *0.05*
12 h3 *0.41*

Perhaps the other rook should have been placed on the d-file, in order to have the c1 square for the bishop. Now it is difficult to do without this move, in view of the threat of ... ♘g4.

In the event of 12 ♘d2 ♘g4 13 ♗xg4 ♗xg4 14 f3 ♗e6 Black has an excellent position. 12 ♘e1 ♘g4 13 ♗xg4 ♗xg4 14 f3 ♗e6 15 b3 ♗f8 16 ♘d3 f6 17 ♖d2 is somewhat better, although here too White cannot really expect any serious advantage.

12 ... **♗f8** *0.18*

This takes control of the a3-f8 diagonal, and especially the c5 square.

13 ♘d2 *0.47*

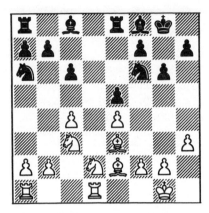

13   ...   b6!?   0.46

An unusual treatment. After nearly half an hour's thought Kasparov rejects the usual ... ♗c5 and ... ♘c5. In the event of 13 ... ♗c5 14 ♗xc5 ♘xc5 15 b4 ♘e6 16 ♘b3 White controls d4 and has a spatial advantage on the queenside. But 13 ... ♘c5 comes seriously into consideration, after which 14 b4 ♘e6 15 c5 is possible.

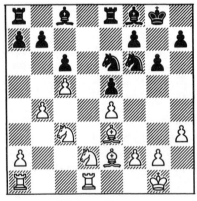

analysis diagram

When making his 13th move, this must have been the continuation that Kasparov wanted to avoid. Indeed, the consequences of the standard 15 ... ♘d4 are extremely unclear; after 16 ♗d3 ♗e6 17 ♗xd4 exd4 18 ♘e2 the d4 pawn may become a target for attack. But Black is not obliged to defend passively. By breaking up White's queenside pawn phalanx with 15 ... b6, he can take the initiative. For example, 16 ♘b3 (*16 cxb6 ♗xb4*) 16 ... a5 17 a3 (*17 cxb6 axb4 or 17 bxa5 bxc5*) 17 ... a4, and Black relieves the pressure. The attempt by White to maintain the pressure with 16 ♘a4 does not achieve anything real, for example: 16 ... bxc5 17 bxc5 (*17 ♘xc5 ♘xc5 18 bxc5 ♗e6*, and Black has no difficulties) 17 ... ♘d7 18 ♖dc1 ♖b8, with an equal game.

14	a3	1.05	♘c5	0.48
15	b4	1.15	♘e6	0.48
16	♘b3	1.19	♗a6	1.12

Black has completed his development, but it is difficult for him to gain active counterplay, since White has set up a solid pawn formation.

| 17 | f3 | 1.26 | ♘h5 | 1.21 |

Threatening 18 ... ♘g3.

| 18 | ♗f2 | 1.31 | ♖ed8 | 1.31 |

18 ... ♖ad8 was stronger and more natural.

| 19 | &fl | *1.33* | ♘hf4 | *1.49* |
| 20 | g3 | *1.43* | ♘h5 | *1.49* |

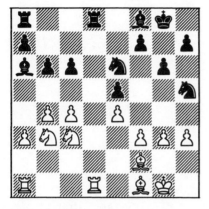

21 ♔g2?! *1.43*

To be considered was de Firmian's suggestion of 21 ♘a4, with the idea of playing c4-c5 and the prospect of gaining the a5 square for a knight. A possible continuation was 21 ...f5 22 exf5 gxf5 23 c5 &xf1 24 ♔xf1 bxc5 (*24 ... b5 25 ♘c3* followed by *♘a5*) 25 ♘axc5 ♘xc5 26 ♘xc5 &xc5 27 bxc5 ♘f6 28 ♖d6, with advantage to White.

21	...		f5	*1.49*
22	♖ab1	*1.47*	♖ac8	*1.56*
23	♖xd8	*2.03*		

Play involving ♘a4 is now too late, e.g. 23 exf5 gxf5 24 ♘a4 &g7 25 c5 &xf1 26 ♔xf1 b5 27 ♘c3 e4.

23	...		♖xd8	*1.56*
24	♖d1	*2.06*	♖xd1	*1.56*
25	♘xd1	*2.06*	fxe4	*2.02*
26	fxe4	*2.06*	c5	*2.03*

The position has simplified and is absolutely level. Neither side has any justification for playing for a win, and the game is clearly approaching its logical conclusion. The mass exchanges which now take place on c5 do not leave this in any doubt.

27	bxc5	*2.13*	♘xc5	*2.04*
28	♘xc5	*2.13*	&xc5	*2.04*
29	&xc5	*2.14*	bxc5	*2.04*

The remainder of the game does not require any commentary.

30	♘c3	*2.14*	♘f6	*2.05*
31	♔f3	*2.14*	&b7	*2.05*
32	&d3	*2.17*	♔f8	*2.10*
33	h4	*2.20*	h6	*2.10*
34	&c2	*2.21*	♔e7	*2.12*
35	&a4	*2.22*	a6	*2.14*
36	♔e3	*2.23*		
	Draw agreed			

GAME SIX   24 October

To the surprise of most of the experts, Karpov, playing the Ruy Lopez again as Black, avoided a further theoretical discussion in the Zaitsev Variation. An explanation for this can be found, we think, in the commentary to Games 2 and 4.

The variation chosen by Black in the present game was introduced into tournament practice by the great Estonian player Paul Keres. Whether Karpov's choice came as a surprise to Kasparov (and after all, this variation had already occurred occasionally in the games of the Ex-World Champion), or whether the reason was Black's innovation on move 15, White did not manage to gain any advantage from the opening. Moreover, soon many of the grandmasters present at the game (they included Ex-World Champion Boris Spassky, who in the past had successfully employed this variation as Black) preferred Karpov's position. This opinion was confirmed by the evaluation of the computer program 'Deep Thought'.

With the white pieces Kasparov, naturally, did not want to play like Black. Seeking the initiative, he resorted to his favourite stratagem – the sacrifice of a pawn. And as a result (true, not without the help of his opponent) he gained more than the initiative – a formidable attack. But in a difficult position, and also in time trouble, Karpov began playing both more strongly and more inventively. Thus at one point he tried to tempt White into winning queen for rook and bishop, after which he was counting on setting up an impregnable fortress. Kasparov did not bother to try testing its solidity. He quite rightly hoped for more, and continued his pursuit of the enemy king. But his play at the finish was inaccurate.

Analysis of the adjourned position established that the World Champion had thrown away the greater part of his advantage with his 41st move (instead of rook to c8 he should have moved his queen), which he could (and should!) have considered without hurrying and then sealed, rather than make on the board.

Kasparov-Karpov
Ruy Lopez

1	e4	*0.04*	e5	*0.00*
2	♘f3	*0.04*	♘c6	*0.01*
3	♗b5	*0.04*	a6	*0.01*
4	♗a4	*0.04*	♘f6	*0.01*
5	0-0	*0.04*	♗e7	*0.01*
6	♖e1	*0.04*	b5	*0.01*
7	♗b3	*0.04*	d6	*0.01*
8	c3	*0.05*	0-0	*0.02*
9	h3	*0.05*	♘d7	*0.02*

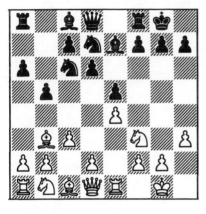

With this move Karpov avoids a repetition of the variation which occurred in Games 2 and 4. Perhaps he was dissatisfied with the outcome of the opening, or perhaps he was afraid of some surprise. And so a new variation comes onto the stage, one which used to occur frequently in tournaments several decades ago.

10 d4 *0.06* **♗f6** *0.02*

Now the point of Black's open-ing set-up is revealed. Surprisingly, its aim – to prevent the classic Spanish manoeuvre ♘b1-d2-f1 – is similar to that on which Black's play was based in Games 2 and 4. But whereas there this was achieved by pressure on the e4 pawn, here it is achieved by the threat to the d4 pawn.

11 a4 *0.06*

It should be mentioned that this attack on the queenside is often carried out by White when he encounters some difficulty in his queenside development. The alternative method of development is 11 ♗e3 followed by ♘bd2, but whether this is any better is the big question.

11 ... **♗b7** *0.03*

Black's last move has to some extent rehabilitated this old variation. At one time 11 ... b4? used to be played here, but after 12 d5 ♘a5 13 ♗c2 bxc3 14 b4 ♘b7 15 a5 White has an overwhelming position. 11 ... ♖b8 12 axb5 axb5 13 d5 is also unsatisfactory for Black.

12 axb5 *0.29*

The fact that Kasparov thought for more than 20 minutes on this move suggests that he had doubts about its advisability at the given moment. The alternatives include 12 ♗e3 ♘a5 13 ♗c2 ♘c4 14 ♗c1, which has occurred most often in practice, and 12 d5 (we consider this the strongest), and only after 12 ... ♘e7 – 13 axb5.

12	...		axb5	0.04
13	♖xa8	0.29	♕xa8	0.06
14	d5	0.29	♘a5	0.16
15	♗c2	0.30		

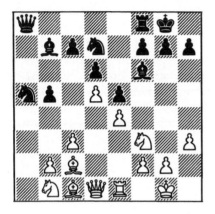

15	...		♘c4!	0.19

This innovation significantly improves Black's game. In the games Tal-Keres (USSR 1964), which continued 15 ... ♖b8 16 ♘a3 ♗a6 17 b4 ♘c4 18 ♘xc4 bxc4 19 ♗a4, and Tal-Stein (USSR 1965), where there followed 15 ... ♗e7 16 ♘a3 c6 17 dxc6 ♗xc6 18 ♕e2 ♕a6 19 ♘d2, White gained an opening advantage.

16	b3	0.38	♘cb6	0.20
17	♘a3	0.42	♗a6	0.21
18	♘h2	1.05		

It is obvious that the knight at

a3 is badly placed, and White, in our opinion, should have been concerned for its future. Especially since fate itself has prepared for it a post at b4, where it will occupy a dominating position. Therefore we suggest the following solution to this problem: 18 ♗b1, planning ♘c2. There is only one way that Black can try to prevent this – by 18 ... ♘c5 (*18 ... c6* fails to *19 dxc6 ♕xc6 20 ♗d2 ♘c5 21 ♘c2!*, when, since taking on b3 is not possible on account of *♘b4*, the aim is achieved). It should also be mentioned that for a long time it will be difficult for Black to make the freeing advance ... c6. True, for White too it is not easy to play actively.

After the text move Black is able to play ... c6.

18	...		c6	0.31
19	dxc6	1.12	♕xc6	0.31
20	♗d2?	1.13		

A loss of time since the knight at a3 now requires defending. It would have been better to defend the c3 pawn with 20 ♕f3.

20	...		♗e7!	0.55
21	♘g4?!	1.15	♖a8!	0.58

Here Black had the interesting possibility of 21 ... f5!?, sharply changing the character of the play. After 22 exf5 ♗b7 and White's best defence 23 ♕f3 ♕xf3 24 gxf3 ♖a8 25 ♘xb5 ♖a2 26 ♘e3 ♗xf3

Black has sufficient initiative for the pawn. But the move played is significantly stronger.

22 ⵥe3 *1.24*

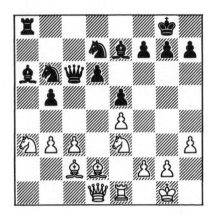

22 ... **ⵥf6** *1.00*

It seems to us that 22 ... ♗b7 would have been much better, attacking the white knight and gaining a strong initiative.

| **23** | **ⵥf5** | *1.32* | **♗f8** | *1.01* |
| **24** | **♗g5** | *1.32* | **ⵥbd7** | *1.02* |

Some commentators criticised Karpov for this move, and recommended the opening of the centre by 24 ... d5. After 25 exd5 ⵥfxd5 it seems to us that, apart from the quiet 26 ⵥb1 (when Black does not achieve anything real, since the pawn cannot be taken, e.g. *26 ... ⵥxc3 27 ⵥxc3 ♕xc3 28 ♖e3 ♕c7 29 ⵥh6+ ♚h8 30 ♕d3 g6 31 ♗f6+ ♚g7 32 ♗xe5 ♗xe5 33 ♖xe5*, with advantage to White),

there are also sharper alternatives. For those who like excitement, we can recommend 26 ♗e4.

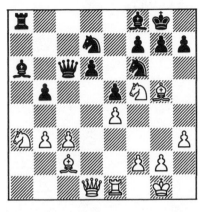

25 c4! *1.33*

White sacrifices a pawn, in return for which his light-square bishop becomes a strong piece.

25	**...**		**bxc4**	*1.13*
26	**bxc4**	*1.39*	**♗xc4**	*1.31*
27	**ⵥxc4**	*1.40*	**♕xc4**	*1.31*
28	**♗b3**	*1.41*	**♕c3?!**	*1.33*

The situation demands of Black very precise play, to avoid ending up in a difficult position. White's pressure fully compensates for the sacrificed pawn. The text move only appears to gain a tempo, and in fact merely loses time. Therefore 28 ... ♕b4 should have been preferred. From this square the queen keeps under attack both the rook at e1 and the e4 pawn. The natural continuation would be 29 ♖e3 ♖a3 *(29 ... ⵥxe4 30 ♗xf7+! ♚xf7*

*31 ♕d5+ ♔g6 32 ♕e6+ ♔xg5 33
h4+ ♔h5 34 ♖xe4 and wins, or
32... ♘df6 33 ♗xf6 gxf6 34 ♕g8+
etc) 30 ♕f3.*

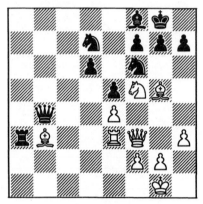

analysis diagram

Black has no need to sacrifice
the exchange (as was thought by
many experts during the game) by
30 ... ♖xb3 31 ♖xb3 ♕e1+ (*31...
♕xe4 32 ♘h6+ gxh6 33 ♗xf6
♕xf3 34 ♖xf3 ♘xf6 35 ♖xf6*, with
the better ending for White) 32
♔h2 ♘xe4 33 ♗e3!, with advantage to White.

In the diagram position Black
has available a powerful counter-
blow in the centre, which substan-
tially changes the evaluation of
the position – 30 ... d5!. It is now
White's turn to think of his own
safety, since after, for example,
31 exd5 ♗c5 32 ♖c3 ♖xb3 33
♖xb3 ♕e1+ 34 ♔h2 ♗xf2 he
loses. The simplest is 31 ♗xf6
♘xf6 32 ♗xd5, when there is

material equality and a drawish-
looking position.

29   ♔h2   1.45

This move is forced, but also
useful, since all the same the white
heavy pieces are intending to move
from the back rank to the third.
But how can Black exploit this
breathing space?

29   ...   h6?!   1.46

Again Black forces White to
'waste' time, and provokes a useful
move. The match bulletin recommends 29 ... g6 30 ♖e3 ♕a1 31
♕d2 gxf5 32 ♗xf6 f4 (*32... ♘xf6?*
loses to *33 ♖g3+ ♗g7 34 ♕g5 ♘e8
35 ♕e7 ♕a7 36 ♗xf7+ ♔h8 37
♕f8+ ♗xf8 38 ♖g8* – a pretty
'helpmate'!), when Black wins a
piece. But instead of 31 ♕d2 in
this variation, we recommend 31
♕f3 gxf5 32 ♕xf5 ♗e7 33 ♗h6
♔h8 34 ♖g3 ♗f8 (*34 ... ♖g8 35
♖xg8+ ♘xg8 36 ♕xf7+ or 36
♕xd7* leads to an advantage for
White) 35 ♗g5 ♗e7 36 ♗xf7 ♖f8
37 ♕e6 ♗d8 38 ♗xf6 ♗xf6 39
♕xd7, or 35 ... ♗g7 36 ♗xf6 ♘xf6
37 ♖xg7 ♔xg7 38 ♕g5+ ♔f8 39
♕xf6 ♕a7 40 h4, in both cases
with advantage to White.

Possibly here too it would have
been easier to gain a draw by
returning the pawn with 29 ... d5,
e.g. 30 ♗xd5 ♘xd5 31 ♕xd5 ♕a5
32 ♕d1 ♘c5. But Karpov does
not like giving up pawns. Possibly

he underestimated the following regrouping of the white pieces, or perhaps he overestimated the possibilities of his own position.

| 30 | ♗xf6 | 2.02 | ♘xf6 | 1.47 |
| 31 | ♖e3 | 2.03 | ♕c7 | 1.52 |

Black switches to passive defence. We recommend active defence by 31 ... ♕b2. Now in the event of 32 ♕f3 there can follow 32 ... ♖b8! 33 ♗c4 (*33 ♘xh6+ fails to 33 ... gxh6 34 ♕xf6 ♖xb3*) 33 ... ♕c1, when 34 ♘xh6+ leads only to a draw: 34 ... gxh6 35 ♕xf6 ♕xc4 36 ♖g3+ ♔h7, and White has to force perpetual check, since after 37 ♕f5+ ♔h8 38 ♕g4 Black wins by 38 ... f6. The basic idea of this defence is all the time to keep the formidable light-square bishop under attack. In the event of 32 ♖g3 there follows 32 ... ♔h8, while if 32 ♖f3 ♖a3.

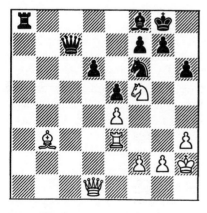

| 32 | ♖f3! | 2.03 |

White regroups in a different way from that which Karpov would have liked. Evidently, like many others, he expected the attack to be continued by 32 ♖g3. However, the latent pressure on the f-file, and in particular on the vulnerable f7 square, is much more effective than the direct attack on the g-file.

| 32 | ... | ♔h7 | 2.18 |

Nothing is changed by 32 ... ♕d8 33 ♘e3 ♔h8 34 ♕d3, with the idea of ♘d5.

33	♘e3	2.05	♕e7	2.25
34	♘d5	2.07	♘xd5	2.25
35	♗xd5	2.07	♖a7	2.25

Thanks to the opposite-colour bishops White has a strong attack (the extra pawn is of no significance here). For his part, Black is ready to give up queen and pawn for rook and bishop (*36 ♖xf7 ♕xf7 37 ♗xf7 ♖xf7*) in the hope of erecting a fortress. But White quite rightly does not go for win of material, and continues to intensify the pressure.

| 36 | ♕b3! | 2.08 | f6 | 2.26 |
| 37 | ♕b8 | 2.10 | g6 | 2.27 |

(see diagram)

| 38 | ♖c3 | 2.16 |

Seirawan's suggestion of 38 g4 would have prevented ... h5, and thus not allowed Black to increase the freedom of his king. Now White

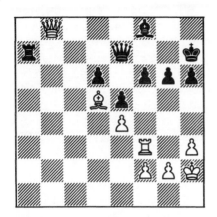

threatens ♖c3 and ♖c8, when if ...
♗g7 he gives mate by ♖h8+, while
after ... ♔g7 he wins the queen by
♖e8. How can Black defend? He
has two possibilities:

(a) 38 ... ♖d7 (with the idea of
driving the white queen off the
8th rank; at this point neither *38
... f5* nor *38 ... h5* is possible) 39
♖c3 ♖d8 40 ♕b6 ♗g7 41 ♖c7
♖d7 (allowing White's heavy
pieces onto the 7th rank is no
better: after *41 ... ♕f8 42 ♕b7*
Black is completely stalemated
and *h4-h5* is decisive) 42 ♖c8, and
White's aim is achieved.

(b) 38 ... ♖c7 39 ♖a3 ♔g7 (*39...
♖d7 40 ♖c3* transposes into the
previous variation) 40 ♖a8 ♖d7
41 ♕b6 ♔h7 42 ♗c6 ♖c7 43 ♖e8
♕g7 44 ♗d5 ♖e7 45 ♖c8, and
against ♕b8 there is no defence.

38	...		h5!	2.27
39	g4	2.17	♔h6	2.28
40	gxh5	2.25		

A positional concession. 40 ♕b6
was steadier, with the aim of pro-
voking an opening of the game on
the kingside. But here, as it turns
out, White acquired the plan of a
direct attack on the king along the
g-file. Only . . . it did not take
place.

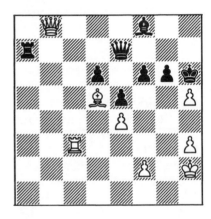

40	...		♔xh5!	2.28
41	♖c8?!	2.26		

A mistake, made after the time
control. White's play along the
8th rank does not succeed, and
the threat of ... f5 forces him to
consider the safety of his own
king. Therefore here he should
have played 41 ♕c8! ♔h6 42 ♖g3
♖d7 (*42 ... ♔h7 43 h4*) 43 ♗c6
♖c7 44 ♕g4 ♕f7 45 ♗d5 ♕e8 46
♗e6 (recommended by Kasparov).

41	...		♗g7	2.29
42	♖e8	2.58		

The sealed move. Kasparov later
offered a **draw**, which was accepted.

GAME SEVEN   26 October

In the 7th game Karpov gained his first win in the match, and the score became level: 3½–3½. But to be fair, the greater part of the responsibility for the result lay with the World Champion: Kasparov made what was perhaps the worst blunder in his career, overlooking an elementary tactical blow.

For the fourth time, playing Black, Kasparov chose the King's Indian Defence. As in the previous games, fairly soon the play took on an original character. From the opening Karpov gained a slight but persistent advantage, and more important – 'his' kind of game, in the style of gradually accumulating slight advantages, which often turn into major difficulties for the opponent.

Kasparov was hardly justified in allowing the exchange of his knight, which had reached the centre by a roundabout way, and which was capable of cementing together Black's position. He preferred to remain with the two bishops, for the activation of which he was forced to further weaken his pawn structure. True, White too did not manoeuvre in the best way possible. It is not clear how it would all have ended, had not Kasparov, in a roughly equal position, played the suicidal 27 ... ♛a5??. "I didn't see anything!", the World Champion replied immediately after the game, when he was asked to 'reinforce' this move with at least some kind of variation-cum-hallucination.

As a result, White transposed into a won ending where he was a pawn up. Through inertia Kasparov made another pseudo-active move with his bishop, which led to further exchanges and simplified White's problems.

The game was adjourned, but the result of it was not in doubt. And indeed, it was not resumed.

Karpov-Kasparov
King's Indian Defence

1	d4	0.00	♞f6	0.00
2	c4	0.00	g6	0.01
3	♞c3	0.00	♝g7	0.01
4	e4	0.00	d6	0.01
5	♞f3	0.01	0-0	0.01
6	♝e2	0.01	e5	0.01
7	♝e3	0.01	♞a6	0.06

The repetition of this eccentric

59

move suggests that it is not accidental, and that it probably contains some subtleties. But it is hard to imagine that these can compensate for the poor position of the knight on the edge of the board.

8 0-0   *0.02*   **♘g4**   *0.06*

Kasparov avoids 8 ... c6, as he played in Game 5. Possibly the course taken by that game did not in some way suit the World Champion.

9 ♗g5   *0.03*   **f6**   *0.06*
10 ♗c1   *0.06*   **♔h8**   *0.08*

An innovation – although this useful prophylactic move has been played in analogous positions.

In the game Cebalo-I.Sokolov, Yugoslavia 1989, Black continued here 10 ... ♛e8, and after 11 h3 ♘h6 12 dxe5 dxe5 13 b3 ♗e6 14 ♗a3 ♖f7 15 ♕c2 ♗f8 16 ♗xf8 ♕xf8 17 a3 ♖d7 18 ♖fd1 ♖xd1+ 19 ♘xd1 ♘f7 the position was equal.

11 h3   *0.19*   **♘h6**   *0.09*

Compare the positions of the white and black knights!

12 dxe5   *0.24*

Typical of Karpov, and in the given instance a perfectly justified decision to clarify the position. Instead of this capture it is hard to find a useful move to maintain the

tension. Now in the event of the natural reply 12 ... dxe5 White could continue 13 b3, and then develop his dark-square bishop at a3, where it is actively placed.

12   ...   fxe5!?   *0.11*

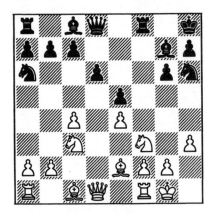

An equally typical decision by Kasparov to give the position an unusual, non-routine character.

What are the plans for the two sides? Black must first transfer his knight from a6 to e6, after which he will have the possibility of play on the kingside, and also the very solid ... c5 followed by ... ♘d4.

White's plan is to attack in the centre and on the queenside, and the essence of the subsequent struggle is the clash of these plans.

13 ♗e3   *0.28*   **♘f7**   *0.11*
14 ♕d2   *0.28*   **♘c5**   *0.21*
15 ♘g5!?   *0.53*

Black is close to the implementation of his plan which was mentioned earlier. But White also had available another interesting possibility: 15 ♗xc5 dxc5 16 ♕e3 b6 17 ♖fd1 ♗d7 18 a3, threatening to begin an attack on the queenside with b2-b4. In the event of 18 ... a5 White gains a clear positional advantage by 19 ♘d5.

| 15 | ... | ♘xg5 | 0.37 |
| 16 | ♗xg5 | 0.53 | ♗f6 | 0.38 |

16 ... ♕e8 looks more logical, leaving the bishop at its lawful place – g7.

17 ♗e3! 0.56

Now ♗xc5 is threatened.

| 17 | ... | ♘e6 | 0.49 |

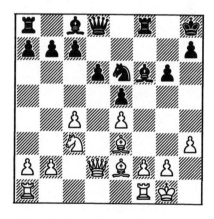

| 18 | ♗g4 | 0.59 | h5? | 1.12 |

A further mistake. By allowing the exchange of his knight for the light-square bishop, Black ends up in a passive position. Of course, after 18 ... ♘d4 19 ♗xc8 ♖xc8 20 ♗xd4 exd4 21 ♘b5 Black would have lost a pawn without any particular compensation. But by playing 18 ... ♘f4! (with the threat of ... ♗xg4 followed by returning the knight to e6) Black would have retained his important knight and obtained a satisfactory position. Kasparov prefers to keep his two bishops.

19	♗xe6	1.00	♗xe6	1.12
20	♘d5	1.03	♗h4	1.12
21	♖ac1	1.14

21 ♗xa7 ♗xd5 22 ♕h6+ ♔g8 23 ♕xg6+ ♔h8 24 ♕xh5+ ♔g8! (but not *24 ... ♔g7? 25 ♗e3!*, winning) would have led to perpetual check.

21	...	♔h7	1.23
22	♖c3	1.25	♖f7	1.27
23	b3	1.27

23 ♖d3 came into consideration, in anticipation of a possible ... c6. For example, 23 ... c6 24 ♘c3 ♗xc4 25 ♖xd6 ♕c7 (*25 ... ♕e7 26 ♖d1 ♗d5 27 ♗c5*) 26 ♖d1 ♗d5 27 ♘b5, and wins.

| 23 | ... | c6 | 1.35 |
| 24 | ♘b4 | 1.28 |

(see diagram)

The white knight is forced to this poor square, since c3 is occupied by the rook. Now White has only a minimal advantage.

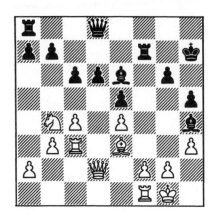

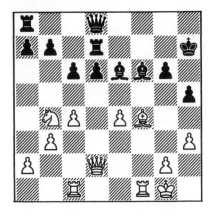

24	...	♖d7	*1.37*
25	♖cc1?	*1.34*	

Here too 25 ♖d3 is more logical.

| 25 | ... | ♗f6 | *1.38* |

At last the bishop returns to the 'King's Indian' diagonal.

| 26 | f4 | *1.38* |

The game becomes sharper, but this opening of the position by White is rather premature. He should have first regrouped his forces.

26	...	exf4	*1.44*
27	♗xf4	*1.38*	

The position is roughly equal. White controls slightly more space, but the two strong bishops are sufficient compensation, especially with the position about to be opened up.

| 27 | ... | ♕a5?? | *1.50* |

With the worst now over for Black, Kasparov makes an incomprehensible blunder. He had a choice between 27 ... ♕e7 and 27 ... ♕h8.

The most surprising thing is that exactly the same elementary oversight was made by Spassky in his match with Fischer at Reykjavik in 1972 (Game 8).

28	♘d5!	*2.03*	♕c5+	*1.51*
29	♔h1	*2.08*		

On 29 ♗e3 there could have followed 29 ... ♗g5! 30 ♘f6+ ♔h6 31 ♗xc5 ♗xd2 32 ♖cd1 ♖dd8, with chances of saving the game.

29	...	♗xd5	*1.52*
30	cxd5	*2.09*	♕d4	*1.56*

30 ... ♕b5 could have led to a position which occurred in the

game: 31 ♗h6 ♗g7 32 ♗xg7 ♔xg7
33 ♕c3+ ♔h7 34 dxc6 bxc6 35
♕xc6 ♕xc6 36 ♖xc6.

31	**dxc6**	*2.10*	**bxc6**	*1.56*
32	**♖xc6**	*2.11*		

39	**♖f4**	*2.20*	**g5**	*2.10*
40	**♖f6**	*2.25*	**♖xe4**	*2.12*
41	**♖xe4**	*2.28*	**♖xe4**	*2.13*
42	**♖xd6**	*2.29*	**♖e7**	*2.14*
43	**♖a6**	*2.33*	**♔g7**	*2.17*

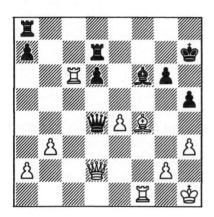

32	**...**		**♖e8**	*1.57*

32 ... ♕xe4 was relatively best, keeping the queens on.

33	**♖c4**	*2.13*	**♕xd2**	*1.57*
34	**♗xd2**	*2.13*	**♗e5**	*2.01*
35	**♗e3**	*2.17*	**♗g3**	*2.03*
36	**♖f3**	*2.19*	**h4**	*2.07*

Kasparov's final mistake. The only way to continue resisting was by keeping the bishops on – 36 ... ♗e5. In the rook ending the pawn at h4 becomes weak.

37	**♗f2**	*2.20*	**♗xf2**	*2.10*
38	**♖xf2**	*2.20*	**♖de7**	*2.10*

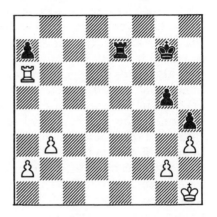

Here the game was adjourned, and two minutes later Karpov sealed his move. The following day Kasparov **resigned** without resuming.

Black must keep his rook at f7, in order to defend the a7 pawn and simultaneously prevent the emergence of the white king. In addition, he is forced to keep his king at g7 or h7, since if it moves to the back rank there follows ♖a5, forcing ... ♖g7, and the white king can come out.

The winning plan is simple: White plays g2-g3, ♔g2, then gxh4 gxh4 and finally ♖a4.

GAME EIGHT   *29/30 October*

This was perhaps the key game in the New York half of the match. It was notable for the intensity of the struggle in all its phases, for its time scrambles and sharp changes of situation, and for the fact that the result remained in doubt to the very end.

It also had its psychological background: how would the World Champion's play be affected by his defeat in the previous game? Statistics were not in his favour: after losing to Karpov in the past, Kasparov had won one game, lost four, and drawn eleven.

Karpov was not averse to seizing the initiative in the match. On move 14 he employed an innovation in the Ruy Lopez, leading to a sharp pawn clash in the centre. After 45 minutes' thought Kasparov found a reply which seemed to catch his opponent unawares; at any event, three moves later it was Karpov who had to think for a long time. However, up to a certain point he defended excellently, but then a mistake allowed Kasparov to build up a strong attacking position. No one doubted that he would convert his advantage into a win. But in his opponent's time trouble Kasparov played uncertainly and planlessly. To crown his misfortunes, before the control he overlooked the loss of a pawn.

The general assessment (this was also later admitted by Kasparov himself) was that White's position was now lost. True, there was still plenty of play in it. Essentially a new game had to be played, one which was to last more than a further five hours. On this occasion Kasparov demonstrated his skill in defence. Restraining his temperament, he patiently conducted a difficult defence, at the same time not allowing the enemy king out of the sights of his long-range pieces. Finally this long-suffering game ended in a draw, and it was after this encounter that many experts predicted that the first half of the match would conclude with the scores level.

	Kasparov-Karpov				2	♘f3	*0.00*	♞c6	*0.00*
	Ruy Lopez				3	♗b5	*0.00*	a6	*0.00*
					4	♗a4	*0.00*	♞f6	*0.00*
1	e4	*0.00*	e5	*0.00*	5	0-0	*0.01*	♝e7	*0.00*

6	♖e1	*0.01*	b5	*0.00*
7	♗b3	*0.01*	d6	*0.00*
8	c3	*0.01*	0-0	*0.00*
9	h3	*0.01*	♘d7	*0.01*
10	d4	*0.02*	♗f6	*0.01*
11	a4	*0.06*	♗b7	*0.01*
12	♗e3	*0.06*		

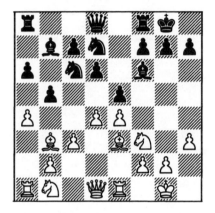

By supporting the d4 pawn White tries to develop his queenside pieces, but this continuation is unlikely to solve his opening problems.

12	...		♘a5	*0.12*
13	♗c2	*0.06*	♘c4	*0.19*
14	♗c1	*0.06*	d5!?	*0.22*

An innovation, which certainly merits consideration. Black has a lead in development, and therefore his desire to open the position is quite reasonable. Although, we think that to rely on the outcome of the opening in Ivanchuk-Karpov (Reggio Emilia 1989/90), as a result of which this innovation

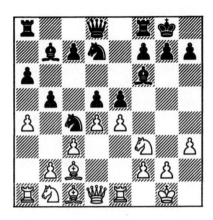

was evidently conceived, would be premature. That game went 14 ... exd4 15 cxd4 c5, extending the influence of the bishop at f6, with the idea of answering 16 b3 with 16 ... cxd4. Ivanchuk played 16 axb5. Now in the event of 16 ... axb5 17 ♖xa8 ♕xa8 18 b3 ♘b6 19 d5 White gains a slight advantage. Karpov continued 16 ... cxd4, but after 17 bxa6 ♖xa6 18 ♖xa6 ♗xa6 19 ♘xd4 White still held an advantage.

| 15 | dxe5!? *0.50* |

The only way of maintaining the tension. Black has an easy game after 15 exd5 ♗xd5 16 b3 ♗xf3 17 ♕xf3 ♘d6.

15	...		♘dxe5	*0.25*
16	♘xe5	*0.50*	♘xe5	*0.28*
17	axb5	*0.55*		

The fact that Karpov thought for rather a long time over his reply suggests that in his preparations he had not considered this exchange to be timely, and that he had mainly reckoned on 17 f4 ♘g6 18 e5. Indeed, White could have made the exchange at any convenient moment. But now Black acquires new possibilities, on the consideration of which Karpov spent 37 precious minutes. Not bad compensation for Kasparov, for his apparently premature exchange, especially since, to all appearances, Karpov did not derive any great benefit from this. For our part, we will endeavour to reveal these possibilities to the reader and to evaluate them.

17	...	axb5	*1.05*

Thus the first possibility was 17 ... dxe4 18 ♕xd8 ♖fxd8 19 bxa6, the advisability of which we reject.

18	♖xa8	*0.55*	♕xa8?! *1.10*

Karpov exploits the second possibility, but, it would seem, to his own detriment. At first sight this continuation is more active than 18 ... ♗xa8, but in fact the pressure on the long diagonal proves ineffective. The main events, as we will soon see, develop on the kingside, and therefore Black should have kept his queen in the centre and played 18 ... ♗xa8.

19	f4	*0.59*	♘g6	*1.11*
20	e5	*0.59*	♗h4	*1.17*
21	♖f1	*0.59*	♗e7	*1.17*

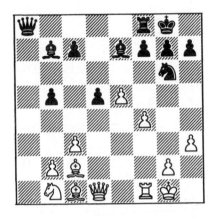

Let us take stock. Black's last manoeuvre ... ♗f6-h4-e7 has parried the immediate f4-f5, but it is clear that the battle will revolve around this advance. As soon as it becomes possible, Black's position will become critical, and it is from this viewpoint that the next few moves of the two players must be considered. It should be mentioned that Black also has available the undermining move ... f6. In short, the position is very tense and the value of every move is extremely high.

22	♘d2!	*1.08*

This developing move is also directed against ... f6. For example, 22 ... f6 23 ♘f3 fxe5 24 f5 ♘h4 25 ♘g5, with a strong attack, in which White exploits the undefended state of the black knight. There can follow 25 ... e4 26 ♕g4 ♗c8 27 ♕xh4 h6 28 ♕g4 hxg5 29 ♗b3 with the threat of ♕xe4. White has a clear advantage.

| 22 | ... | ♗c5+ | *1.47* |

Karpov was criticised for this move, and instead 22 ... d4 was recommended, greatly sharpening the situation. But his decision is understandable. After 23 cxd4 White's centre is strengthened, and if the complications after 23 ... ♗xg2 24 ♖f2 do not give a positive result, Black will quickly lose. The suggested follow-up was 24 ... ♘h4, and now:

(a) 25 ♕g4. This is not considered in the match bulletin. If now the bishop moves from g2, there follows 26 f5, which settles matters. And after the possible 25 ... f5 26 exf6 ♗xf6 27 ♖xg2 ♗xd4+ 28 ♔h2 White easily defends, retaining a material advantage. For example, 28 ... ♖xf4 29 ♕e6+ ♔h8 30 ♖e2.

(b) 25 f5 ♗g5, and the bulletin states that Black has everything in order. However, let us continue this variation: 26 ♕g4 ♗xd2 27 ♗xd2 ♕a1+ 28 ♕d1 ♕xd1+ 29 ♗xd1 – the remainder is a matter of technique.

| 23 | ♔h2 | *1.11* | d4 | *1.56* |
| 24 | ♕e2 | *1.36* | | |

There was no point in going in for the complications of 24 ♘b3 ♗b6 25 cxd4 ♗xg2.

| 24 | ... | dxc3 | *2.01* |

| 25 | bxc3 | *1.41* | ♖d8 | *2.05* |
| 26 | ♘e4 | *1.49* | ♗a3 | *2.12* |

Up till now Karpov has defended splendidly. Now he had to parry the threat of ♘g5, which could have been done in two ways. He could either take the knight with 26 ... ♗xe4 when, although White's position is better, nothing decisive is apparent, or else retreat with 26 ... ♗e7!?.

27	♗xa3	*1.57*	♗xe4	*2.25*
28	♕xe4!	*1.59*	♕xa3	*2.25*
29	f5	*2.01*	♘e7	*2.25*

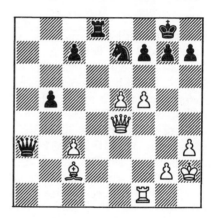

| 30 | ♕h4? | *2.04* |

A loss of time. Sooner or later the rook will have to be moved to the third rank, where it defends the c3 pawn and takes part in the attack on the king, and here 30 ♖f3! looks very strong. Now the method of defence employed by Karpov in the game, 30 ... f6, does not work in view of 31 ♖g3 ♔h8

32 exf6 gxf6 33 ♗b3!. This position deserves a diagram.

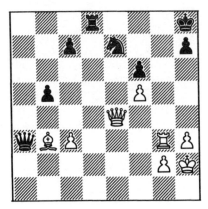

analysis diagram

Black cannot take the bishop: 33 ... ♕xb3 34 ♕xe7 etc. The threat of ♕g4 can only be parried by 33 ... ♘g8, but then comes 34 ♕e6, concluding matters after 34 ... ♕d6 35 ♕f7 ♕f8 36 ♖xg8+.

There only remains 30 ... ♕c5. Then both 31 ♖d3 and 31 ♗b3 look horrible for Black. 31 ♖g3 ♕d5 32 ♖d3 ♕a8 33 ♖d7 is also strong. Everywhere White wins quickly.

30   ...   f6!   2.26

The only possibility of continuing the resistance. 30 ... ♕c5 was bad on account of 31 f6 ♕xe5+ 32 ♔h1 ♘g6 33 ♗xg6 hxg6 34 fxg7.

31   ♕g3   2.12

But now on 31 ♖f3 there could

have followed 31 ... ♔h8, with good chances of a defence. The subsequent events took place in a time scramble, and therefore to try to analyse and explain what happened on the board would be simply foolish. All that can be said is that, although Kasparov had only a little more time, in search of his lost advantage he tried to devise something. As for the Ex-World Champion, he relied entirely on his intuition, and it did not let him down.

31	...		♔f8	2.27
32	♔h1	2.18	♕c5	2.28
33	exf6	2.19	gxf6	2.28
34	♗b3	2.19	♘d5	2.28
35	♕h4	2.20	♔g7	2.28
36	♖d1	2.24	c6	2.28
37	♖d4	2.25	♕xc3	2.29
38	♖g4+	2.25	♔h8	2.29
39	♗xd5	2.26	♕a1+	2.29
40	♔h2	2.26	♕e5+	2.29

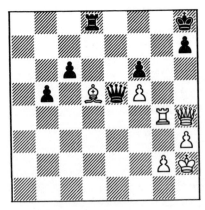

Here the smoke of battle cleared,

the time scramble ended, the game was adjourned, and it transpired that Karpov was a pawn up with winning chances. It should be said that the exposed position of Black's king makes it extremely difficult to realise his material advantage. On the resumption we gained another opportunity to assess the work of the two opponents' analytical teams. Black's first problem is to protect his king and create the threat of advancing his pawns.

41	♖g3	2.34	cxd5	2.29
42	♕g4	2.35	♕c7	2.30
43	♕d4	2.36	♕d6	2.30
44	♔h1!	2.37		

On 44 ♕g4 there follows 44 ... ♕d7, when the threat to the f5 pawn prevents an attack on the f6 pawn.

| 44 | ... | | ♖e8 | 2.41 |
| 45 | ♕g4 | 2.37 | ♕d7 | 2.42 |

By a series of manoeuvres Karpov has broken up White's battery on the g-file. Now ... d4 is threatened, and this can only be prevented by the text move. But what next? For the moment it is not apparent how either of the pawns can be advanced.

| 46 | ♖d3 | 2.37 | ♖e1+ | 2.53 |
| 47 | ♔h2 | 2.37 | ♖e4 | 3.07 |

Now, of course, White cannot take on e4, because Black inter-

poses a check at c7.

| 48 | ♕g3 | 2.38 | ♖e5 | 3.13 |

Now the pawn at f5 is hanging, so that White's next move is forced.

| 49 | ♖a3 | 2.46 | ♖e8 | 3.20 |
| 50 | ♕f4 | 2.49 | | |

Creating the threat of ♖a6.

| 50 | ... | | ♕b7 | 3.24 |

50 ... d4 did not work in view of 51 ♖a6 d3 52 ♖d6 ♕c7 53 ♕d4 ♖e5 54 ♖d8+ ♖e8+ 55 ♖d6 with a draw. In passing, ... ♕b8 is threatened.

51	♔h1	3.03	♕b8	3.24
52	♕h4	3.03	♕b6	3.26
53	♕b4	3.06	d4!?	3.29

The attempt to drive the white rook to a passive position by 53 ... ♕f2 54 ♖a1 (bad is *54 ♕xb5 ♖e1+ 55 ♔h2 ♕f4+ 56 ♖g3 ♖e3*, and wins) 54 ... ♖g8 55 ♖g1 ♕e2 would not have achieved much after 56 ♕c5.

54	♖g3	3.13	♕c7	3.29
55	♖d3	3.15	♕c1+	3.29
56	♔h2	3.15	♕f4+	3.29

Karpov's second time trouble comes to an end, and he could now have taken a look around. But to save time on the clock he repeats the position once more.

57	♔g1	3.15	♕c1+	3.58
58	♔h2	3.16	♕f4+	3.58
59	♔g1	3.16		

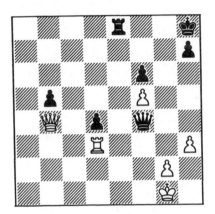

Black has significantly improved the placing of his pieces, and has advanced his pawn to d4. Nevertheless, a win is still not apparent. Perhaps the best chance was to go into a queen ending, which could have been forced by 59 ... ♔g7!? (threatening 60 ... ♖e2) 60 ♖xd4 ♖e1+ 61 ♕xe1 ♕xd4+ 62 ♔h1 b4. But Karpov wants more.

| 59 | ... | | ♖c8 | *4.02* |
| 60 | ♖d1 | *3.17* | ♖d8 | *4.04* |

Karpov decides to give up a pawn, and rely on his far-advanced d-pawn.

61	♕xb5	*3.22*	♕e3+	*4.04*
62	♔h1	*3.24*	d3	*4.04*
63	♕a5	*3.43*	♕d4	*4.04*
64	♕a1!	*3.43*	♕b6	*4.08*

On 64 ... ♕d6 there would have followed 65 ♖xd3!. Black manages

to advance his pawn to d2 only in a rook ending, where this is no longer of any significance.

65	♕a2	*3.53*	♔g7	*4.10*
66	♕d2	*3.55*	♕c5	*4.19*
67	♖f1	*4.03*	♖d4	*4.21*
68	♖f3	*4.07*	♕d6	*4.22*
69	♖e3	*4.08*	♖a4	*4.24*
70	♖e1	*4.10*	h5	*4.26*
71	♖b1	*4.17*	♕d7	*4.28*
72	♕d1	*4.21*	♔h6	*4.29*

In *Sovietsky Sport* Tal writes that Black missed a good opportunity: 72 ... ♕d4 73 ♕xh5 ♖a1. It was an opportunity, but not a very serious one, since White gives an elementary perpetual check: 74 ♕g6+ ♔f8 75 ♕h6+ ♔e7 76 ♕g7+ ♔d6 77 ♕f8+ ♔e5 78 ♕e7+ ♔xf5 (*78 ... ♔xf5 79 ♕c7+ ♔e3?? 80 ♕g3+, and White even wins*) 79 ♕h7+ ♔e5 (*79 ... ♔e6 80 ♕g8+ ♔e5 81 ♕g3+ ♔d5 82 ♕g8+*) 80 ♕e7+ etc.

73	♕d2+	*4.32*	♔g7	*5.01*
74	♕e3	*4.38*	h4	*5.03*
75	♕f3	*4.39*	♔h6	*5.08*
76	♕e3+	*4.40*	♔g7	*5.11*
77	♕f3	*4.40*	d2	*5.16*
78	♕h5	*4.41*	♕f7	*5.16*
79	♕xf7+	*4.41*	♔xf7	*5.16*
80	♖d1	*4.42*	♖d4	*5.17*
81	♔g1	*4.43*	♖d5	*5.17*
82	♔f2	*4.44*	♖xf5+	*5.17*
83	♔e2	*4.44*	♖g5	*5.18*
84	♔f2	*4.44*	**Draw agreed**	

GAME NINE   31 October

The amazing constancy of themes chosen by the players for their theoretical discussions in New York – 'King's Indian' and 'Ruy Lopez' – was finally broken. In this game Kasparov switched to the Grünfeld Defence, on which he had relied heavily in the previous two matches. Karpov's supporters judged this to be a psychological mini-success, since the Ex-World Champion had happy memories of this opening.

In this game too Kasparov can hardly have been content with the outcome of the opening. Besides, Karpov of course had some opening preparation in store. Despite the early exchange of queens, White gained a persistent positional advantage and attacking possibilities. Black did not gain any active counterplay, and was forced to switch to prolonged passive defence. Kasparov was all the time prepared to give up a pawn, after which the position would have become clearly drawish thanks to the opposite-colour bishops. But just the opposite occurred. Karpov committed a transposition of moves, after which Kasparov happily (and with relief) 'ate up' White's central pawn. Journalists immediately called Karpov's fatal move the worst in the match. We should mention, however, that this blunder did not lead to defeat for the Ex-World Champion, as occurred with Kasparov in Game 7, and he got away with merely a slight fright. After the 'horrors' experienced, the two players were so agitated that they forgot their alienation, and immediately after the draw was agreed they began animatedly discussing what had happened. It seemed that both were content with the happy ending in this game.

Karpov-Kasparov
Grünfeld Defence

1	d4	0.00	♘f6	0.00
2	c4	0.00	g6	0.00
3	♘c3	0.00	d5	0.00

Thus the King's Indian takes a rest, and is replaced by the Grün-

feld Defence, which Kasparov had already employed several times in the previous matches.

4	cxd5	0.01	♘xd5	0.00
5	e4	0.01	♘xc3	0.00
6	bxc3	0.01	♗g7	0.01
7	♗e3	0.01	c5	0.02

71

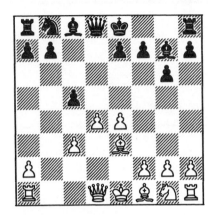

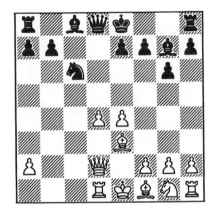

8 ♕d2 0.04

Karpov was undoubtedly prepared for the Grünfeld Defence. The fact that he spent a few minutes on this last move suggests to us that at this point he also had other moves in his arsenal. One variation, 8 ♗c4 ♘c6 9 ♘e2 0-0 10 0-0 ♗g4 11 f3 ♘a5 12 ♗xf7+ ♖xf7 13 fxg4, was employed several times in the 1987 match. The text move has the idea of removing the rook from the diagonal raked by the dark-square bishop, making it possible to advance d4-d5. In recent years this continuation has acquired some popularity.

8	...		cxd4	0.20
9	cxd4	0.05	♘c6	0.21
10	♖d1	0.15		

(see diagram)

10	...		♕a5	0.23

It seems to us that Black could have delayed this move and played 10 ... 0-0, continuing 11 ... ♕a5 only in the event of 11 d5. If 11 ♘f3 then he has the useful move 11 ... ♗g4. Therefore White can continue 11 ♗e2. Here, apart from 11 ... ♕a5 12 ♕xa5 ♘xa5 13 ♘f3, which transposes into the present game, Black can also try 11 ... e5!?. After 12 d5 ♘d4 13 ♘f3 ♘xe2 14 ♕xe2 ♕a5+ 15 ♗d2 ♕a4 16 0-0 both 16 ... b6 and 16 ... ♗d7 lead to interesting positions (the queens have not been exchanged!).

11	♕xa5	0.34	♘xa5	0.23
12	♘f3	0.34		

The alternative method of development, 12 ♗d3 0-0 13 ♘e2, did not achieve a lot in Yusupov-Gulko, Linares 1989.

12	...		0-0	0.25
13	♗e2	0.54	♗d7	0.39
14	♗d2	1.03	b6	0.42

15 0-0 *1.08* **♖fd8!?** *1.05*

Of course, 15 ... ♖fc8 would have led most simply to the drawing haven, but Kasparov, performing as usual in the role of 'disturber of the peace', and not wanting to agree to a slightly inferior position, tries to sharpen the game. But the position is such that Black is not able to change the character of the play – all the same he is obliged to defend.

16	♖c1	*1.20*	♗g4	*1.18*
17	d5!	*1.23*	♘b7	*1.23*
18	h3	*1.30*	♗xf3	*1.24*
19	♗xf3	*1.30*		

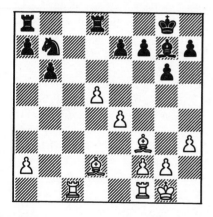

19 ... **♘c5?!** *1.31*

Kasparov plans a defence on the dark squares, but is in too much of a hurry. He should first have exchanged one pair of rooks, after which it would have been easier to defend. Therefore 19 ... ♖ac8 was essential, after which

neither 20 ♗g4 ♖xc1 21 ♖xc1 ♘c5 22 ♗b4 ♗d4, nor 20 ♗b4 ♘c5 21 ♖c4 ♗e5, nor 20 ♗e3 ♗b2 21 ♖c6 ♘a5 promises White any real advantage. Now, however, Black finds himself in difficulties.

| 20 | ♗e3 | *1.38* | ♖ac8 | *1.34* |
| 21 | ♗g4 | *1.42* | ♖b8 | *1.34* |

It seems to us that 21 ... ♖c7 was better, when it is hard for White to achieve anything real. For example, 22 ♗f4 ♖b7, and Black can base his defence on ... e5. Of course, White will not win the pawn on c5, since after 22 ♗xc5 bxc5 23 ♖xc5 Black develops pressure on f2 and obtains sufficient counterplay.

22	♖c4!	*1.46*	h5	*1.35*
23	♗f3	*1.46*	e6	*1.36*
24	♖d1	*1.51*	exd5	*1.38*
25	exd5	*1.51*	♗e5	*1.42*
26	g4	*1.57*	hxg4	*1.58*
27	hxg4	*1.57*		

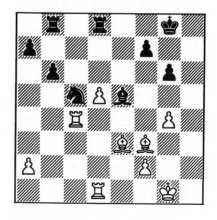

27 ... ♘b7? 1.58

Whereas up till now Black had made only some slight errors, this last move is probably a decisive mistake. He should have based his defence on the idea of a pawn sacrifice. Therefore he should have transferred his rook from b8 to a more active position; this could have been achieved by 27 ... ♖b7.

28	♖a4	2.01	♘a5	2.01
29	g5	2.10	♖bc8	2.02
30	♗e2	2.10		

Not allowing the knight to come into play.

30	...		♗d6	2.10
31	♔g2	2.17		

With the idea of switching the heavy pieces to the h-file. 31 ♗a6 was also good, for example 31 ... ♖c2 32 ♔g2 ♗c5? 33 ♗d3 ♖b2 34 ♗xc5, or 31 ... ♖c7 32 ♔g2 ♘b7? 33 ♗xb7 ♖xb7 34 ♗d4 ♗f8 35 ♗f6 ♖d6 36 ♖h4 ♗g7 37 ♖dh1, and in each case White wins.

31	...		♗c5	2.19

(see diagram)

32 ♗d2?? 2.20

An incomprehensible blunder, which robs Karpov of the fruits of his subtle play. He should have combined the advance of his d-pawn with mating threats. The

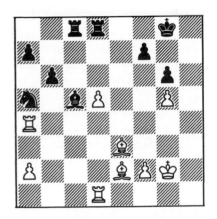

main defender of Black's king is his bishop, and the only thing that Karpov had to decide was on which square to exchange it.

We suggest the following variation: 32 ♗f4! ♗d6 33 ♗xd6 ♖xd6 34 ♖h4 ♖c5 (*34 ... ♔g7 35 ♖dh1 ♖g8 36 ♖h7+ ♔f8 37 ♖c1 etc*) 35 ♗f3 (*35 ♖dh1 ♔f8 36 ♗f3 is already possible, but Black can sacrifice the exchange with drawing chances*), and now: (a) 35 ... ♖c4 36 ♖h3 ♘b7 37 ♖dh1 ♔f8 38 ♖h8+ ♔e7 39 ♖e1+ ♔d7 40 ♗e2 ♖b4 41 a3, or (b) 35 ... ♖d8 36 ♖dh1 ♔f8 37 ♖h8+ ♔e7 38 ♖e1+ ♔d7 39 ♖h7 ♖f8 40 ♖e6, and Black loses material.

32	...		♖xd5	2.23
33	♗f3	2.23	♖dd8	2.27
34	♗xa5	2.27	**Draw agreed**	

The opposite-colour bishops make this result inevitable.

GAME TEN

After the game Kasparov was sceptical about the strength of Karpov's 8th move innovation in the Petroff. Perhaps this was why he did not look very carefully for a refutation of Black's idea, spending only ten minutes on his reply. On the other hand, over 11 ♗g5 he thought for 37 minutes and, as he himself soon realised, this move was merely a waste of time. This factor naturally affected the World Champion's mood. And yet the main reason why, as early as move 18, and still with the better position (this was his evaluation after the game), Kasparov offered a draw, and Karpov readily accepted it, was that both were tired after the two exhausting previous games.

Kasparov-Karpov
Petroff's Defence

1	e4	0.00	e5	0.00
2	♘f3	0.01	♘f6	0.00
3	d4	0.04		

Usually Kasparov has continued 3 ♘xe5 d6 4 ♘f3 ♘xe4 5 d4.

3	...		exd4	0.01

This can perhaps also be considered a new move. From Karpov one might have expected 3 ... ♘xe4, which has been played by his trainers Makarychev and Mikhalchishin. It can be assumed that this is the result of the Hungarian grandmaster Lajos Portisch joining the Karpov team.

4	e5	0.05	♘e4	0.04
5	♕xd4	0.06	d5	0.04

6	exd6	0.06	♘xd6	0.04
7	♘c3	0.14	♘c6	0.07
8	♕f4	0.15	♘f5!	0.09

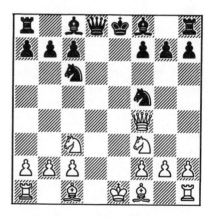

But this is a genuine innovation. Modern theory recommends here 8 ... g6 9 ♗e3 ♗g7 10 ♗d3 0-0 10 0-0-0 ♗e6 12 ♗c5, with a spatial advantage. 8 ... ♗e7 or 8 ... ♗e6 is

75

also possible. It is amazing that in such a well-analysed opening as Petroff's Defence, with a history of some one hundred and fifty years, it is possible on move eight to find a continuation not mentioned by theory. The effect of this move lies in not only its novelty, but also its serious positional basis. It should also be mentioned that, out of the eight moves made by Black, this is the fourth by one knight alone. But White's strongest piece, which has been brought out into the centre, can now be attacked by the black minor pieces.

9   ♗b5   *0.25*

This move does not look logical. White pins the knight, which is not threatening his queen. 9 ♗c4 or 9 ♗d2 would have been more natural. But the most thematic was 9 ♕e4+, only bringing out the bishop to b5 after 9 ... ♗e7. The transposition of moves allows Black to develop his bishop at d6 and to block the check with his queen.

9   ...   ♗d6   *0.14*
10   ♕e4+   *0.26*   ♕e7   *0.18*

The match bulletin gives the variation 10 ... ♘e7 11 ♗f4 ♗f5 12 ♕e3 ♗xf4 13 ♕xf4 ♗xc2 14 ♘d4, with the initiative for the pawn. But instead of 13 ... ♗xc2, 13 ... 0-0 is stronger: 14 ♗xc6

bxc6 15 ♘d4 ♕d6, with only a slight advantage to White.

11   ♗g5   *1.03*

An unnecessary move, since the reply ... f6 merely helps Black. The immediate 11 ♗d2 was somewhat better.

11	...		f6	*0.29*
12	♗d2	*1.03*	♗d7	*0.29*
13	0-0-0	*1.13*	♕xe4	*0.39*
14	♘xe4	*1.13*	♗e7	*1.13*

15	g4	*1.17*	a6	*1.35*
16	♗c4	*1.21*		

A more promising continuation was 16 ♗xc6 ♗xc6 17 ♖he1 ♗xe4 18 ♖xe4 ♘d6 19 ♖e2 ♔f7 20 ♘d4 ♖he8 21 ♘e6 ♗f8 22 ♖de1 ♖e7 23 f4! g6 24 ♗b4 ♖c8 25 b3, with a marked advantage.

16	...		♘d6	*1.35*
17	♘xd6+	*1.21*	♗xd6	*1.35*
18	♖de1+	*1.37*	**Draw agreed**	

GAME ELEVEN   5 November

After the rather brief and insipid 10th game (a clear exception to the series of interesting encounters), chess fans were again expecting a tense and fascinating struggle in the 11th. Kasparov reverted to the King's Indian Defence. True, on this occasion he avoided the eccentric knight move to the side of the board (7 ... ♘a6) in favour of a tried and tested continuation. However, as transpired during the game, it had been tested insufficiently thoroughly. On his 13th move (a lucky number for the World Champion!) Kasparov sacrificed the exchange. Interestingly, this idea (which is not mentioned in any of the numerous opening books) was found by him in his preparations for the 7th game. But then, when he was leading, Kasparov had decided not to risk employing it. Indeed, at first sight Black did not obtain any particular gains in return. Many grandmasters (Benjamin, Krogius) were categorical: "Black has no compensation!". Only the 'professional' King's Indian players sensed, rather than saw: "Black has some play!". Kasparov continued as though nothing had happened, without forcing matters. Gradually Black's threats began to grow. In a complicated position a forcing variation 'turned up', with a bishop and rook sacrifice by Black ending in perpetual check to the white king. Both players readily went in for this continuation, although each had the opportunity to deviate.

The experts are increasingly of the opinion that the two players have decided not to tempt fate, and will transfer the weight of the struggle from America to 'their own' European continent.

Karpov-Kasparov			2	c4	0.00	g6	0.00
King's Indian Defence			3	♘c3	0.00	♗g7	0.01
			4	e4	0.00	d6	0.01
1	d4	0.00	♘f6	0.00	5	♘f3	0.00	0-0	0.01

| 6 | ♗e2 | 0.00 | e5 | 0.01 |
| 7 | ♗e3 | 0.02 | exd4 | 0.01 |

In this variation Black can very quickly make the central break ... d5, which leads to a double-edged game.

| 8 | ♘xd4 | 0.02 |

After 8 ♗xd4 there follows 8 ... ♘c6, when the bishop has to retreat.

8	...		♖e8	0.02
9	f3	0.08	c6	0.02
10	♕d2	0.08		

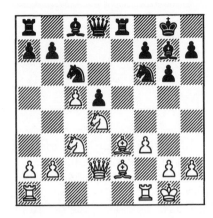

A more cautious continuation here is 10 ♗f2 d5 11 exd5 cxd5 12 c5, but both players are evidently aiming for one and the same position, which theory evaluates in favour of White. However, Kasparov, like many other supporters of the King's Indian Defence, has a different opinion regarding this.

10	...		d5	0.02
11	exd5	0.11	cxd5	0.02
12	0-0	0.11	♘c6	0.02

12 ... dxc4 has also been played. The game Savon-Geller, 37th USSR Championship, Moscow 1969, continued 13 ♗xc4 a6 14 ♖ad1 b5 15 ♗b3 ♗b7 16 ♗h6! ♗xh6 17 ♕xh6 ♘bd7 18 ♘e4!, and White gained a strong attack.

| 13 | c5 | 0.23 |

This is the position for which both players were aiming.

| 13 | ... | | ♖xe3!? | 0.05 |

A typical Kasparov exchange sacrifice. Of course, this continuation had been prepared beforehand. But it was not a matter of calculating any specific variations; the sacrifice has a clear positional basis. Left without an opponent, the 'King's Indian bishop' becomes terribly strong, and the exchange is a small price to pay for this.

The usual continuation here is 13 ... ♕e7, when Olafsson-Gligorić, Havana 1966, went 14 ♗f2 a6 15 ♘xc6 bxc6 16 ♗d3 ♗e6 17 ♘e2 a5 18 ♘d4, with a great advantage to White.

For those who like excitement we should also mention the game Tolush-Geller, Moscow 1950: 13 ... ♕e7 14 ♗f2 ♕xc5 15 ♘e6 ♕xf2+!? 16 ♖xf2 ♗xe6 (does not this remind you of the queen sacrifice for two minor pieces in the 3rd game of the present match?).

14 ♕xe3 *0.28* **♕f8!** *0.05*

The results of Black's operation are already apparent – now 15 ... ♘g4 is threatened. White cannot maintain the blockade at d4; his next move is practically forced.

15 ♘xc6 *0.50* **bxc6** *0.05*

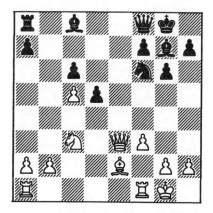

Despite White's material advantage, his position is very insecure. He has to worry about his weak c5 pawn, Black's pressure on the b-file, and his weakness on the dark squares. In addition, Black's pawn at d5 ensures him good prospects in the centre. Therefore the initiative is with Black, and he has at least equal chances.

16 ♔h1 *0.53*

A useful prophylactic move. Karpov does not yet know what actions his opponent will undertake, and he makes a move which will in any event prove useful.

16 ... **♖b8** *0.10*

With this move Black to some extent reveals his cards prematurely. It seems to us that first ... ♗f5 or ... ♗e6 should have been considered, with the idea of combining play in the centre with pressure on the kingside.

17 ♘a4 *0.59*

This move is forced. 17 ♖ab1 fails to 17 ... ♗f5 18 ♗d3 d4 19 ♕xd4 ♖d8.

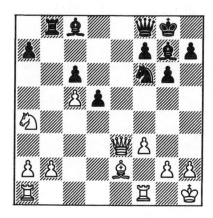

17 ... **♖b4** *0.19*

The start of a fantastic plan, in which the rook is transferred to h4, where it will take part in a direct attack on the enemy king. Here too 17 ... ♗f5 came into consideration.

18 b3 *1.00* **♗e6** *0.41*

As we see, Kasparov makes a sensible pause. Now the coordinating 19 ... ♛b8 is threatened, after which the attack develops of its own accord. For example, 19 ♖ad1? ♛b8 20 ♛f2 ♞h5, threatening ... ♗e5.

19 ♞b2! _1.20_ **♞h5** _0.56_

The transfer of the white knight to d3 forces Kasparov, without completing his preparations, to take immediate action. The development of events is now largely forced.

20 ♞d3 _1.28_ **♖h4** _0.58_
21 ♛f2 _1.31_ **♛e7** _1.00_

This leads to a draw. 21 ... g5 would have led to unclear play: 22 g3 ♗d4 23 gxh4 (_23 ♛e1? ♖xh2+! 24 ♔xh2 ♛h6 and wins_) 23 ... ♗xf2 24 ♖xf2 gxh4 with the better chances for Black, or 22 g4 ♗xa1 (_22 ... ♞f6 23 ♛g3 d4_, with a double-edged game, also looks tempting) 23 ♖xa1 ♞g7, and Black's chances are certainly not worse.

22 g4 _1.36_

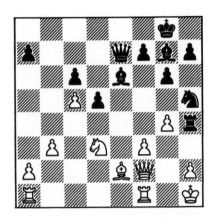

22 ... **♗d4!** _1.01_
23 ♛xd4 _1.45_

White cannot play 23 ♛g2 in view of the simple 23 ... ♗xa1 24 ♖xa1 ♛f6 25 ♖e1 ♞f4, when Black has the better game.

23 ... **♖xh2+!** _1.02_
24 ♔xh2 _1.47_ **♛h4+** _1.02_

Draw agreed, in view of perpetual check.

GAME TWELVE   *7 November*

Kasparov, playing White, had a last chance to bring some happiness to his supporters – by general opinion, it was with him that the sympathy of a majority of American fans lay. The Ruy Lopez was again played, but instead of 12 axb5 (Game 6) or 12 ♗e3 (Game 8), Kasparov chose 12 ♘a3. But Karpov was armed 'to the teeth' – here too a prepared line was awaiting the World Champion – 12 ... exd4!. One senses that the Challenger has prepared with his team for this match like never before.

The game proceeded with alternating fortunes. The play of the super-grandmasters clearly bore the stamp of fatigue. Kasparov displayed unaccustomed indecisiveness at the board. But Karpov too, after seizing the initiative towards the end of the game, did not risk sacrificing the exchange, which was considered the strongest continuation.

On the threshold of time trouble the players prudently agreed a draw in a complicated position. A draw in the game, and a draw in the first half of the match: 6-6. Karpov seemed happy with such an intermediate outcome, but Kasparov was obviously disappointed. His over-optimistic pre-match forecasts had for the moment not been confirmed in practice.

Kasparov-Karpov
Ruy Lopez

1	e4	*0.01*	e5	*0.00*
2	♘f3	*0.01*	♘c6	*0.00*
3	♗b5	*0.01*	a6	*0.01*
4	♗a4	*0.01*	♘f6	*0.01*
5	0-0	*0.01*	♗e7	*0.01*
6	♖e1	*0.02*	b5	*0.01*
7	♗b3	*0.02*	d6	*0.01*
8	c3	*0.02*	0-0	*0.01*
9	h3	*0.03*	♘d7	*0.01*
10	d4	*0.03*	♗f6	*0.02*
11	a4	*0.04*	♗b7	*0.02*

Fifty per cent of the games played in New York by Karpov with Black have been with this variation. Jumping ahead, it should be mentioned that the present game too ends in a draw, and so it can be considered that this defence has proved reliable. But is this really so?

12   ♘a3?! *0.04*

This at first sight strange move is Kasparov's third attempt to gain an opening advantage in the

81

given position. The drawback to the move is clearly apparent – with the centre not blocked, a knight on the edge of the board can hardly be usefully employed. Karpov's reaction is obvious and natural.

12	...	exd4	*0.13*
13	cxd4	*0.05*	

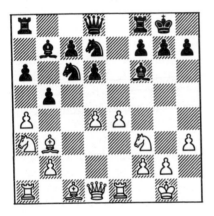

13	...	♘a5?!	*0.16*

Of course, the virtue of this premature move lies not only in its 'cooperative' joint actions with the knight at a3. The idea is to put pressure on e4. After the correct 13 ... ♖e8, with the same idea, White would be faced with the difficult problem of developing his queenside. Thus his dark-square bishop can move only to f4, otherwise one of the central pawns is lost (*14 ♗d2 ♘xd4; 14 ♗e3 ♖xe4*). After 14 ♗f4 ♘a5 15 ♗c2 b4 16 ♘b1 c5 17 ♘bd2 (*17 ♗xd6 b3!*) 17

... cxd4 Black has a good game. 14 ♗c2 is possibly better for White, but after 14 ... ♘b6 15 b3 b4 16 ♘b1 (*16 ♘c4 ♘xc4 17 bxc4 ♘a5*, with satisfactory play) 16 ... ♘xd4 17 ♘xd4 c5 18 ♗b2 cxd4 19 ♗xd4 ♖c8 it is only he who has any difficulties. Black also has an easy game after 14 ♗a2 bxa4 15 ♕xa4 ♘b6 16 ♕d1 ♘b4 17 ♗b1 c5.

14	♗a2	*0.07*	b4	*0.19*
15	♘c4	*0.07*	♘xc4	*0.21*
16	♗xc4	*0.08*	♖e8	*0.22*

By 'successfully' exchanging White's inactive piece, Karpov has handed the initiative to his opponent. Here 16 ...d5 17 ♗xd5 ♗xd5 18 exd5 ♘b6 19 ♗f4 ♘xd5 20 ♗e5 ♖e8 21 ♖c1 would have led to an inferior and passive position. The move played, although more dangerous for Black, offers him more counterchances.

17	♕b3	*0.20*	♖xe4	*0.23*
18	♗xf7+	*0.22*	♔h8	*0.24*

The resulting position is not at all easy to evaluate. The basic drawback for Black is the poor position of his king. His main hopes are associated with his pawn majority in the centre and on the queenside, which may tell, especially in the endgame. White has the more solid position and a definite initiative. If he should succeed in quickly seizing control of the e-file, he will have real chances of an attack on the enemy king. Therefore Kasparov's next move provoked considerable discussion.

19 ♗e3! 0.47

On several chess principles, 19 ♗d2 suggested itself. Analysing the game later in a calm situation, we endeavoured to understand the choice of the Champion. Various explanations and different variations could be put forward, including even the following: 19 ... c5 20 ♖xe4 ♗xe4 21 ♖e1 ♗xf3 22 ♖e8+ ♕xe8 23 ♗xe8 ♖xe8 24 ♕xf3 ♗xd4, and for the sacrificed queen Black undoubtedly has compensation. It could have been thought that the decisive factor in White's choice was a psychological one. Everyone is accustomed to Kasparov sacrificing his queen, yet here the 'disturber of the peace' is his opponent, who until now has not appeared in this role! But everything proved to be

much simpler. After 19 ... a5 20 ♖xe4 ♗xe4 21 ♖e1 d5 22 ♗xd5 the unexpected rejoinder 22 ... ♘c5 sharply changes the situation.

19 ... ♖e7 0.38

The best defence. Weaker is 19 ... a5 20 ♗d5 ♗xd5 21 ♕xd5 ♖e8 (21 ... ♖e7 is very strongly met by 22 ♗g5) 22 ♘g5, with a clear advantage.

20 ♗d5 0.50 c6 0.46

20 ... ♗xd5 transposes into the variations just given.

21 ♗e6 0.56 ♘f8! 1.13

This exclamation mark relates to Black's last three moves, by which Karpov has parried White's immediate threats of ♗g5 and ♘g5.

22 ♗g4 1.23 a5 1.16

Despite Black having found the best defence, the changes which have occurred in the position are to White's advantage. First, thanks to the move ... c6 Black's light-square bishop has been blocked in and his d6 pawn weakened. And second, the black knight has been driven to a passive position. Therefore we think that Kasparov should have adhered to the plan about which we have already spoken, and which, incidentally, up till now he has been implementing – seizing control of the e-file and building up an attack on the king. This plan could have been continued with 23 &f4, exploiting the weakening of the d6 pawn. Without pretending to the absolute truth, we give an example of how events might develop: 23 ... ♘g6 (a logical move, surely?) 24 ♖xe7 &xe7 (if *24 ... ♘xe7, then 25 ♕e6 or 25 ♘g5*) 25 &g3, or 24 ... ♕xe7 25 ♖e1 ♕d8 26 &g3, and in all of these variations White has a significant advantage.

23 h4 also came into consideration, forcing Black once again to parry the threats of both ♘g5 and &g5, when 23 ...h6 can be met by 24 h4, with the threat of &f4.

23 ♖ac1 *1.30*

To judge by this rather colourless move, Kasparov had lost the thread, and White's next few moves convince us of this still further.

23	...		♘g6	1.28
24	&h5	1.36	♖c8	1.37
25	&g4	1.50	♖b8	1.41
26	♕c2	1.51	♖c7	1.54

With the idea of manoeuvring the knight to d5. True, this voluntarily concedes the e-file, which could have been of decisive importance. 26 ... ♕g8 or 26 ... ♕f8 was better. But Karpov, sensing the opponent's uncertainty, decides immediately to 'take the bull by the horns'. At the same time he

sets a little trap . . .

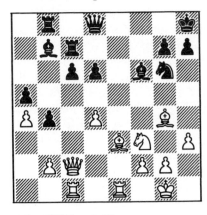

27 ♕f5? *1.59*

. . . into which Kasparov falls. We think that he was hoping not so much to 'grab' the a5 pawn as to gain time for 28 ♘g5 or 28 &g5. But this could have been achieved by the simple positional move 27 ♕d2!, after which Black has these possibilities: 27 ... ♘e7 28 ♘g5 &xg5 29 &xg5, or 27 ... c5 28 ♘g5! cxd4 29 &xd4 &xd4 (*29 ... &xg5 30 ♖xc7! &xd2?? 31 &xg7+ ♔g8 32 &e6 mate*) 30 &e6 ♖xc1 31 ♖xc1, in each case with a clear advantage to White.

27 ... **♘e7!** *1.54*

This is the whole point. The a5 pawn is immune in view of 28 ... ♘d5, when there is no defence against ... ♖a8, winning the queen.

28 ♕d3 *2.00*

With this move White hands

the initiative to his opponent. However, 28 ♕h5, which experts in the foyer were analysing, would also not have achieved anything, in view of 28 ... g6 29 ♗g5 ♘f5! (it is dangerous to accept the queen sacrifice: *29 ... gxh5 30 ♗xf6+ ♔g8 31 ♗e6+ ♔f8 32 ♘g5*, with a certain draw at least) 30 ♗xf6+ ♕xf6 31 ♕g5 ♕xg5 32 ♘xg5 ♘xd4 33 ♖ed1 ♘b3 34 ♖c2, with roughly equal chances.

It seems to us that White could have continued 28 ♕e6. After 28 ... ♘d5 29 ♗g5 Black still has difficult problems to face, in view of the insecure position of his king. The following is an interesting variation: 29 ... h6 30 ♗xf6 ♕xf6 31 ♕xd5!? cxd5 32 ♖xc7, with a strong attack for White.

28	...	♘d5	*2.05*
29	♗d2	*2.00* c5	*2.09*
30	♗e6	*2.03*	

30 dxc5 dxc5 31 ♘e5 came into consideration.

30	...	♘b6	*2.13*
31	dxc5	*2.10* dxc5	*2.21*
32	♕xd8+	*2.11* ♖xd8	*2.21*

In the endgame, as we have already remarked, the advantage is with Black, who on the queenside has a pawn majority and a superior pawn formation. Kasparov now has to act very precisely, to avoid ending up in a lost position.

| 33 | ♗f4 | *2.11* | ♖e7 | *2.23* |
| 34 | ♘g5 | *2.11* | ♗d5 | *2.26* |

The tempting 34 ... ♘xa4 would have been refuted by 35 ♗b3!.

35	♗xd5	*2.23*	♖xd5	*2.26*
36	♖xe7	*2.24*	♗xe7	*2.26*
37	♖e1	*2.24*		

Here, rather short of time, the players **agreed a draw**. Black's position is still slightly better. He has the advantage on the queenside, but White has sufficient counterplay in view of the insecure position of the black king. The following analysis shows that both players were right:

37 ... ♗f8 38 ♘e6 (we consider these the best moves) 38 ... ♔g8 39 b3 ♖d3 (after *39 ... c4 40 ♗c7* Black ends up in a difficult position) 40 ♗c7 ♘d5 41 ♗xa5, and playing for a win leads Black into difficulties: 41 ... ♖xb3 42 ♖d1.

GAME THIRTEEN   24 November

Thanks to the level score in New York, all twelve games were played there, and so the second, Lyon half of the match began with Game No. 13. It was preceded by a small opening ceremony. To the strains of a march, the two participants came onto the stage of the *Palais des Congrès*, illuminated by bright spotlights and the flash-guns of numerous photographers. Behind the chess table, sparkling with gold and diamonds, stood the prize of the jewellery firm "Korloff" destined for the winner of the match. Valued at a million dollars, it would seem to significantly reduce the probability of the match ending in a draw. Blinded by the lights and diamonds, the players sat down at the board, and the Mayor of Lyon, Michel Noir, a passionate chess fan who has done much to have the ancient game included in the school curriculum, started the clocks.

The lengthy break, the level score, the new surroundings, the opening ceremony – all this resembled the start of a new match. But events on the board showed that it was a continuation. Up to move 10 the players repeated the 9th game. There a pawn exchange in the centre occurred at d4, here it was at d5. Black managed to mobilise his pieces well and obtained good prospects. But Kasparov hurried matters, and with a clever exchange sacrifice Karpov extinguished Black's growing initiative. Kasparov answered with a similar sacrifice, and the game went into an ending where Black had to reckon both with White's protected passed pawn, and with weaknesses in his own position. Kasparov found a way to gain active counterplay, and the game, although adjourned, was not resumed.

An interesting statistic is that not one of No. 13 match games between Kasparov and Karpov has given a decisive result – all have been drawn.

Karpov-Kasparov
Grünfeld Defence

					3	♘c3	0.00	d5	0.00
					4	cxd5	0.00	♘xd5	0.00
					5	e4	0.00	♘xc3	0.00
					6	bxc3	0.00	♗g7	0.00
1	d4	0.00	♘f6	0.00	7	♗e3	0.03	c5	0.02
2	c4	0.00	g6	0.00	8	♕d2	0.03	0-0	0.02

86

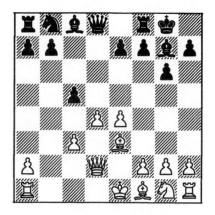

With this move Kasparov deviates from the continuation chosen by him in the 9th game – 8 ... cxd4 9 cxd4 ♘c6 10 ♖d1 – and gives a different direction to the play. There, it will be remembered, the game very quickly went into an ending. Here, obviously, Kasparov is aiming for a more complicated battle.

9 ♖c1 *0.11*

Defending c3 beforehand, which makes it possible to advance d4-d5 at any time.

10 ... ♕a5 *0.08*
10 ♘f3 *0.30* e6 *0.10*

This move, which had already occurred in previous games, is directed against d4-d5.

11 d5 *0.43*

Sooner or later the pressure on d4 will force White to take measures

of some kind. For example, the game Blees-Mikhalchishin, Budapest 1990, continued 11 ♗d3 ♖d8 12 ♗g5 (bad is *12 0-0 cxd4 13 cxd4 ♕xd2 14 ♗xd2 ♘c6*) 12 ... f6 13 ♗e3 cxd4 14 cxd4 ♕xd2+ 15 ♔xd2, and White stood better. Karpov, wishing to clarify matters straight away, plays d4-d5 immediately and, of course, does not gain any advantage.

11 ♗h6 comes into consideration, as played in the 15th game.

11 ... exd5 *0.13*
12 exd5 *0.43* ♖e8 *0.18*

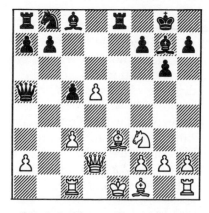

Black has a comfortable game. His queenside minor pieces will soon take up good attacking positions: the bishop will aim for f5, and the knight for f6 or b6. White has only one strategic trump – the passed pawn at d5, which after a possible c3-c4 will also become protected. But this will only really become an advantage when many pieces have been exchanged, i.e. mainly in the endgame. Hence the possible long-term and immediate plans of the two sides: Black must aim for piece play, and White for simplification. It is interesting to note that all this is in accordance with the styles of the two players, and therefore an interesting battle can be expected.

13 &e2 0.53

Could 13 c4 have been played? Of course, after 13 ... ♕xd2+ White has everything in order. But after 13 ... ♕a3, if White plays 14 &d3 (not allowing the enemy bishop to go to f5) 14 ... &g4 15 ♘g5 ♘d7! (of course, Black should not follow Spassky's recommendation in the match bulletin of *15 ... h6 16 ♘e4*, leading to a position which even such an authority as the Ex-World Champion did not try to evaluate, but left us in the dark) 16 0-0 ♘e5 17 &b1 (*17 &e2 h6*) 16 ...b6, Black has the better game.

13	...		&f5	0.27
14	0-0	0.56	♘d7	0.28
15	h3	1.18		

A prophylactic move, parrying the manoeuvre ... ♘f6-g4.

Up till here the game has developed as in Piket-Korchnoi, Wijk aan Zee 1990, which continued 15 ♕b2 ♘f6, with the initiative for Black. In passing, it should be mentioned that White cannot play 15 ♘h4? on account of 15 ... &e4 16 f3 &xd5.

15 ... ♘b6 0.42

Kasparov directs his knight towards a4. This move was criticised by a number of commentators. Some recommended 15 ... ♘f6, others 15 ... h5, and Spassky even suggested 15 ... b5!?. After this nothing is achieved by 16 ♘h4 &e4 17 f3 &xd5 18 ♕xd5 ♘b6 19 ♕xc5 ♖ac8, when Black regains his piece and the knight at h4 remains out of play. And on 16 c4 Black can even play 16 ... b4. Therefore it seems to us that the Ex-World Champion's recommendation merits serious consideration.

16	g4	1.31	&d7	0.46
17	c4	1.31	♕xd2	0.59

It would be unwise to keep the queens on, since after 17 ... ♕a3 there would follow 18 ♖b1, and on the queenside it is difficult for Black to play actively.

| 18 | ♘xd2 | 1.32 | ♘a4 | 1.03 |

In the resulting ending Black has some advantage, since his pieces are significantly more active. It is not easy for White to defend.

19 &f3 1.32

With this last move White has taken control of e4, in order to use this square for his knight.

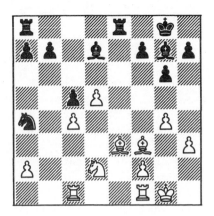

Also, in some cases the advance of the d-pawn is threatened. Black, in turn, should have parried these threats, an aim which would have been satisfied by one of two moves.

The first is the direct 19 ... f5. Then 20 d6 leads to a sharp game after 20 ... ♗e5 21 ♗xb7 ♖ab8 22 ♗d5+ ♔g7, but Black regains the pawn, remaining with a significantly more active position. The quiet 20 ♗f4 would possibly have set Black more difficult problems; against this one can recommend either the quiet 20 ... ♗e5 or the more aggressive 20 ... ♘c3.

The second possibility is 19 ... ♗e5 20 ♘e4 ♖ac8 (or *20 ... b6*) 21 ♗g5 ♔g7, or 21 ♗g2 f5.

19 ... ♘c3? *1.08*

This looks like a blunder. It seems to us that Kasparov simply did not consider White's reply.

20 ♖xc3! *1.42* **♗xc3** *1.08*

21 ♘e4 *1.42* **♖xe4!** *1.13*

In the event of 21 ... ♗g7 22 ♘xc5 White has an obvious advantage.

22 ♗xe4 *1.43*

Here a draw could have been agreed. We think that both players were perfectly well aware of this, but this was the first game in Lyon and they did not want so quickly to disappoint the spectators. The remainder of the game resembles a sparring session, and therefore we will conclude our analysis here.

22	...		♖e8	*1.13*
23	♗d3	*1.44*	b6	*1.14*
24	♔g2	*1.45*	f5	*1.18*
25	gxf5	*1.52*	♗xf5	*1.19*
26	♗xf5	*1.55*	gxf5	*1.19*
27	♖d1	*2.03*	♔f7	*1.28*
28	♖d3	*2.04*	♗f6	*1.29*
29	♖a3	*2.12*	a5	*1.30*
30	♖b3	*2.12*	♗d8	*1.35*
31	♖c3		♗c7	*1.45*
32	a4	*2.21*	♔f6	*1.48*
33	♔f1	*2.23*	f4	*1.53*
34	♗c1	*2.24*	♔f5	*1.55*
35	♖c2	*2.25*	♖g8	*2.00*
36	♖e2	*2.26*	♗e5	*2.01*
37	♗b2	*2.26*	♗d4	*2.01*
38	♗xd4	*2.28*	cxd4	*2.02*
39	♖e7	*2.28*	d3	*2.05*
40	♔e1	*2.28*	♖c8	*2.05*
41	♔d2	*2.32*	♖xc4	*2.08*

The sealed move was **42 ♔xd3**. **Draw agreed** on Karpov's proposal.

To everyone's surprise, in his first 'White' game in Lyon Kasparov chose the Scotch Game. This opening occurred in encounters at the highest level . . . one hundred years ago – in Steinitz's matches with Zukertort (1886) and Chigorin (1892). Romantic chess had passed into the age of *Informator* and chess computers!

This opening had never before occurred in Kasparov's games. But was this choice a surprise for the Ex-World Champion? The all-knowing computers promptly supplied the information: Karpov had defended against the Scotch Game seven times, and very successfully: +3 –0 =4. An excellent score, especially if account is taken of the fact that his opponents included players such as Korchnoi, Timman, Ljubojević and Sax. But to judge by the time taken, Karpov nevertheless had problems.

Of course, the World Champion had found some new ideas in this ancient opening. Very early in the game he sacrificed a central pawn, firstly, to avoid theoretical paths, and secondly, to begin active play as soon as possible. Black, in turn, chose a plan of active counterplay, returning the pawn but achieving a powerful centralisation of his forces.

This was a genuinely open game. For the first time in the match, both kings, which had castled on opposite sides, came simultaneously under mating threats. The two opponents played brilliantly. One recalls how the clever switching of the white queen from one flank to the other via its deep rearguard (32 ♕f1!) was applauded by the experts in the press centre.

One of the World Champion's seconds, Zurab Azmaiparashvili, rated this encounter the best in the match.

Kasparov-Karpov
Scotch Game

1	e4	0.00	e5	0.00
2	♘f3	0.00	♘c6	0.00
3	d4	0.01		

The time machine controlled by Kasparov takes us back to the 19th century – to the age of romantic chess. As we will see, this does not save us from lengthy opening variations. Nowadays this variation of the Scotch Game is employed most often with White by Ljubojević and Timman. It should be mentioned that another player with considerable experience in it, although as the defender, is Anatoly Karpov. *ChessBase* contains seven games played by the Ex-World Champion as Black in this variation.

3	...		exd4	0.05
4	♘xd4	0.01	♘f6	0.10
5	♘xc6	0.01	bxc6	0.10
6	e5	0.01	♕e7	0.10
7	♕e2	0.01	♘d5	0.10
8	c4	0.04	♗a6	0.12
9	b3	0.05	0-0-0	0.37

This position has occurred in numerous tournament games, the first occasions evidently being roughly one hundred years ago: Blackburne-Zukertort, London (match) 1881, and Mieses–Teichmann, Hastings 1895. Until the present time the position has been considered sound for Black, and not without reason – he is ahead in development and White still has to spend several tempi in evacuating his king from the centre. The one drawback to Black's position is the fact that, for the moment, his light-square bishop is shut out of play. And, of course, it was interesting to find out what the World Champion wanted to demonstrate.

10	g3	0.05

At first we thought that this was the innovation of the century,

but then it was discovered that this right belongs to Ljubojević's move 10 ♕b2 in his game against Seirawan, Wijk aan Zee 1986, where after 10 ... ♘b6 11 ♗e2 ♖e8 12 ♗f4 g5 13 ♗g3 ♗g7 14 ♘c3 f5 15 f4 gxf4 16 ♗xf4 ♗xe5 White simply lost a pawn. The source game went 10 ♗b2, and only after 10 ... ♘b6 – 11 g3.

10	...		♖e8	0.50
11	♗b2	0.05	f6	0.50

If he wished, by 11 ... ♘b6 Karpov could have transposed into the Mieses-Teichmann game mentioned above. But Teichmann had no such choice, since there a different move order occurred.

12	♗g2	0.05	fxe5	0.56
13	0-0	0.08		

Let us take stock. Black has won a pawn, but his light-square bishop is still shut in, and there are pawn weaknesses in his king's position. It is this that constitutes White's compensation for the pawn. Here, apart from the text move, Black could have played the prophylactic 13 ... ♘f6, but Karpov is aiming for activity.

| 13 | ... | h5 | *1.05* |

After this White immediately regains his pawn.

14	♕d2	*0.10*	♘f6	*1.07*
15	♕a5	*0.25*	♗b7	*1.07*
16	♗a3	*0.25*		

In the event of the immediate 16 ♕xa7 Kasparov possibly did not like 16 ... ♕c5 17 ♕a4 (after the exchange of queens Black would have a clear advantage) 17 ... ♕b6 followed by ... ♗c5.

16	...	♕e6	*1.19*
17	♗xf8	*0.25*	♖hxf8	*1.23*
18	♕xa7	*0.28*	♕g4!?	*1.42*

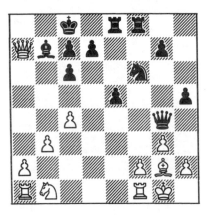

The black queen also takes up an advanced position. By all the classical laws Black stands excellently. The majority of his pieces are centralised and he has available various ways of developing an offensive. White has only his queen in play, and in order to create concrete threats it requires urgent help. At first sight it appears impossible to do this, but it comes by perhaps the only possible route.

| 19 | ♘a3! | *1.21* |

How many times in this match has Kasparov played his knights to the edge of the board, for which he has usually been condemned. But here this move has a very concrete aim. For example, if 19 ... ♕d4, attempting to eliminate White's attack, then 20 c5 ♕b4 (♘c4-a5 was threatened) 21 ♘c4 ♕b5 22 ♖fe1, attacking the e5 pawn and threatening ♗f1. In this way Black's attempt to exchange queens is parried.

| 19 | ... | h4 | *1.49* |

Karpov has no intention of defending passively, and he too aims quickly to create threats against the white king. From this point the play becomes exceptionally critical, since to each move of the opponent's the best reply must be found.

| 20 | ♘c2 | *1.22* |

Now 20 c5 fails to 20 ... hxg3 21 hxg3 ♕h5, when Black is ahead of his opponent.

20	...	**h3!**	*1.53*
21	♗h1	*1.24* ♘e4!	*1.55*

The white king, surrounded by its own pieces, has ended up in a mating net.

22 a4! *1.34*

Kasparov includes a new resource in the attack. Other measures leave Black with the advantage. For example:

(a) 22 ♘b4 ♘c3 23 ♖ae1 ♕d4;

(b) 22 ♖ae1 ♘d2 23 ♘e3 ♘f3+ (*23 ... ♕d4 is also good*) 24 ♗xf3 ♕xf3;

(c) 22 ♕e3 ♘g5, and finally:

(d) 22 f3 (the main alternative) 22 ... ♘xg3 23 ♖f2 (*23 fxg4?? ♘e2 mate*) 23 ... ♕g6 24 hxg3 ♕xg3+ 25 ♔f1 e4 26 fxe4 (*26 ♕e3 exf3 27 ♖xf3 ♕h2!* is unsatisfactory since Black regains his piece, while if *26 ♖e1 exf3 27 ♖xe8+ ♖xe8 28 ♗xf3 h2*) 26 ... ♕d3+ 27 ♔g1 (*27 ♔e1 c5 28 ♕xc5 ♖xf2 29 ♕xf2 ♗xe4*) 27 ... ♖f6 28 ♕e3 ♖g6+ 29 ♔h2 ♕d6+ 30 ♕f4 (*30 ♖f4 ♖g4 31 ♖f1 g5*) 30 ... ♖f8!.

After the text move a5-a6 is threatened, and this obliges Black to force matters.

22	...	♘c3	*2.10*
23	♖ae1	*1.44* ♘e2+	*2.12*
24	♖xe2	*1.44* ♕xe2	*2.12*
25	♘b4	*1.47*	

If Black was aiming for a draw, his next move was a mistake. Here, as long as the white knight

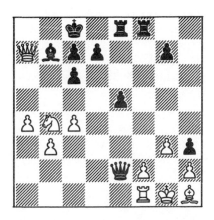

is at b4, it does not help to play 25 ... ♔d8, with the idea on 26 ♕xb7 of forcing a draw by perpetual check with the rook sacrifice 26 ... ♖xf2, in view of 27 ♕b8+ ♔e7 28 ♘xc6+ bxc6 29 ♕xc7+ ♔e6 30 ♕xc6+ ♔e7 31 ♕c5+, and on the next move the rook at f2 can be picked up. Therefore the knight must first be forced to move from b4. This aim is best served by 25 ... ♖f3, attacking the b3 pawn. Now White is obliged to hurry, and after 26 ♘a6 ♔d8! 27 ♕xb7 ♖xf2 the game ends in a draw by perpetual check. This would have been a worthy finish!

26	...	**d5?!**	*2.15*

Now the position is opened up, and this, in our opinion, is to White's advantage, since his bishop joins the attack.

26	cxd5	*1.51*	cxd5	*2.25*
27	♗xd5	*2.16*		

27 ♘xd5 ♕a6 would have been worse. White also does not achieve anything by including his rook in the attack – 27 ♖c1, in view of 27 ... ♕d2 28 ♕c5 ♖f7 29 ♘xd5 ♕d4.

27	...		♗xd5	2.25
28	♘xd5	2.16	♕c2	2.25
29	♕a6+	2.18	♔d7	2.25
30	♘e3	2.19	♕e4	2.25

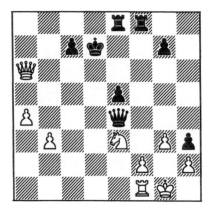

A position which is not easy to evaluate. For the sacrificed exchange White has a pawn, and the black king does not have a safe shelter.

31 ♖c1?! *2.21*

White wants to win the h3, c7 or e5 pawn, which will secure him a stable advantage. 31 ♖d1+ would also have accorded with this aim, but would have been more accurate. Then play is more or less forced: 31 ... ♔e7 32 ♕f1 ♖d8 33

♖e1. Loss of material for Black is inevitable, and White also secures the safety of his king. There is a curious trap after 33 ... ♖d3 34 ♘c4?? ♖xg3+! 35 hxg3 h2+. The correct continuation is 34 ♘g4!.

31	...		♖b8!	2.27

In severe time trouble Karpov finds the only way not only to stay 'afloat' but also to create counterplay.

32 ♕f1 *2.21*

White cannot get by without eliminating the h3 pawn, which is holding his king in a mating net.

32	...		♖xb3	2.27
33	♕xh3+	2.23	♔d8	2.28
34	♕h5	2.26	♔c8	2.28
35	♕d1?	2.27		

After allowing the sacrifice on e3 it is White who has to think in terms of drawing, whereas with 35 ♘c4 he would have retained chances of an attack and could still have tried for a win without particular risk.

35	...		♖xe3	2.28
36	fxe3	2.27	♕xe3+	2.28
37	♔h1	2.27	♕e4+	2.28
38	♔g1	2.27	♕e3+	2.28
39	♔h1	2.27	♕e4+	2.28
40	♔g1	2.28	♖d8	2.29

41 ♕c2 was the sealed move. **Draw agreed** on Kasparov's proposal.

GAME FIFTEEN   28 November

Up to move 11 the players repeated the 13th game. Who had prepared an improvement in the Grünfeld Defence, and where? It turned out to be Ex-World Champion . . . Boris Spassky. In the official match bulletin, where the 13th game was annotated, it was he who accompanied 11 d5 with the brief comment: "I would have preferred 11 ♗d3 or 11 ♗h6." Karpov took this recommendation seriously, whereas Kasparov, to all appearances, did not pay sufficient attention to it. And he regretted this. Without his dark-square bishop, Black's position, despite the exchange of queens, became increasingly dangerous. Karpov skilfully combined threats on both flanks. After the strong 21 ♖h2!, a move which was difficult to find, the World Microcomputer Champion 'Mephisto' evaluated White's positional advantage as being worth a whole pawn.

Aiming for active counterplay, Kasparov replied with a pawn thrust in the centre, which Spassky called "hara-kiri". "Mephisto" demonstrated the winning variation for White, beginning with 26 ♖h4!, suggesting that computers can play certain positions at the level of grandmasters.

Even so, for Black this was the best practical chance. The position became sharper. And chess players, in contrast to computers, have nerves, and fatigue can accumulate. Karpov failed to find the correct continuation, and the initiative and the advantage passed to Black. But Kasparov too, fatigued by his difficult defence, was unable to appreciate fully the change of situation in his favour, and a draw was agreed.

	Karpov-Kasparov								
	Grünfeld Defence				4	cxd5	0.04	♘xd5	0.01
					5	e4	0.04	♘xc3	0.01
					6	bxc3	0.04	♗g7	0.01
					7	♗e3	0.05	c5	0.01
1	d4	0.03	♘f6	0.00	8	♕d2	0.05	0-0	0.02
2	c4	0.03	g6	0.00	9	♘f3	0.15	♕a5	0.03
3	♘c3	0.04	d5	0.00	10	♖c1	0.20	e6	0.04

95

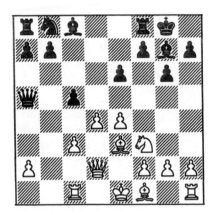

11   ♗h6   0.20

An innovation! (At any event it does not appear in *ChessBase*.) By threatening an attack on the king, Karpov forces his opponent to go into an endgame.

11   ...   ♘c6   0.45
12   h4   0.31

This move obliges Black to relieve the tension in the centre.

12   ...   cxd4   0.47
13   ♗xg7 0.32   ♔xg7   0.47
14   cxd4 0.32   ♕xd2+ 1.03
15   ♔xd2 0.33

This fairly simple position is certainly, in our opinion, attractive to the Ex-World Champion. The point is not just that White, thanks to his strong pawn centre, has a minimal advantage, but rather that here the character of the play suits Karpov more than his opponent. And one more factor. It has

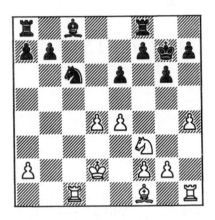

often been said in jest that Kasparov's queen is stronger than Karpov's queen, and from this point of view the exchange of the strongest piece is to Karpov's direct advantage.

15   ...   ♖d8   1.03
16   ♔e3   0.33   ♗d7   1.03
17   ♖b1!? 1.04

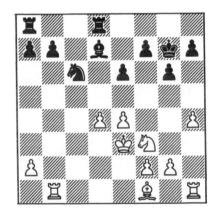

This apparently unpretentious move was the outcome of prolonged thought. The aim of it is clear: not to allow the queen's rook to go to c8. At the same time, c1 is vacated for the king's rook.

17 ...   ⌶ab8?! *1.06*

17 ... ♘a5!? looks more natural, but Kasparov had bad memories of this move from Game 9. On 17 ... b6 White has the unpleasant 18 ♗a6.

18   ♗d3   *1.10*   **♘e7?!**   *1.38*

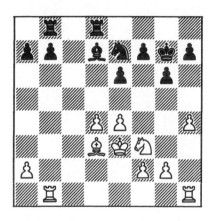

Kasparov takes the pressure off the d4 pawn and deprives himself of counterplay. He should have considered prophylaxis, directed against h4-h5: 18 ... h6 or even 18 ... h5.

19   h5!   *1.39*

Of course, 19 ⌶hc1 was also good, but Karpov justifiably reasons that the threats to the black king will soon become fairly unpleasant, and that it will not be easy for Kasparov to parry them.

19	**...**		**f6**	*1.39*
20	**hxg6**	*1.44*	**hxg6**	*1.41*
21	**⌶h2**	*1.45*	**b6**	*1.56*
22	**g4**	*1.52*		

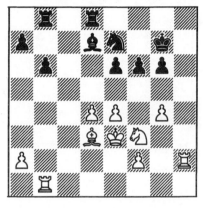

22   ...   e5?   *2.02*

What is this – a gesture of despair? Or an overestimation of Black's position? At any event, he now ends up in a very difficult situation.

Perhaps the only possibility, by the laws of classical chess, was 22 ... g5. Here is a variation showing how, in our opinion, events could have developed: 23 e5 ♘d5+ 24 ♔d2 ⌶h8 25 ⌶bh1 ⌶xh2 26 ⌶xh2 ⌶h8 27 ⌶xh8 ♔xh8 28 ♗e4 ♔g7 29 ♗xd5 exd5 30 exf6+ ♔xf6 31 ♘e5. The ending obviously favours White, although Black retains saving chances.

23	dxe5	2.01	♗xg4	2.02
24	exf6+	2.01	♔xf6	2.03
25	♘d4	2.01	♖b7	2.12

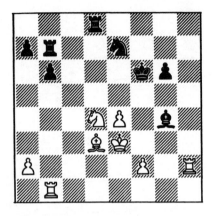

26   f3?   2.09

The computer *Mephisto*, as well as several commentators (for example Miguel Najdorf, who telephoned one of the authors from Argentina), produced the solution 26 ♖h4!, which would have quickly led to a crushing win. Here are the variations: 26 ... ♖bd7 *(26 ... ♗c8 27 f4)* 27 e5+! ♔xe5 *(27 ... ♔g5 28 ♖xg4+! ♔xg4 29 ♖g1+ with a quick mate)* 28 ♖b5+ ♘d5+ 29

♖xd5+ ♖xd5 30 ♘c6+ ♔f6 31 ♘xd8 ♔g5 32 ♖h8.

26	...		♖bd7	2.14
27	♖b4	2.11	♗e6	2.17

Passions have died down, and it is now Karpov who has to act very carefully.

28	♖c2	2.16

In the match bulletin Spassky cites Watson's recommendation of 28 f4!?. However, no variations and no evaluations are given, evidently hinting that White still has the advantage. But after 28 ... ♗g8 it is unlikely that White can count on anything, for example 29 ♖c2 ♖e8 30 ♔f3 ♖ed8.

There now followed a further five moves, and then the players agreed a draw.

28	...		a5	2.20
29	♖a4	2.16	g5	2.20
30	♗b5	2.17	♖d6	2.20
31	♗e2	2.22	♗d7	2.21
32	♖ac4	2.23	♖e8	2.22
33	♖b2	2.26	♘d5+	2.23

Draw agreed

GAME SIXTEEN   1, 2 & 4 December

Journalists in the press centre exchanged meaningful glances when the move 3 d4 was reproduced on the monitor. Again the Scotch Game! This meant that the appearance of this romantic opening in the Champion's repertoire was no accident. True, Alexander Roshal, Deputy Editor of the magazine *64* (and its editor, we would remind you, is Karpov), sceptically shrugged his shoulders: "If Kasparov wants to win the match using the Scotch! . . ." The rest was clear without being said: "then he must be in a bad way."

Black's initial moves, made quickly and with exaggerated confidence, seemed to bear out these words. Although he was soon obliged to part with a pawn, the correct follow-up (16 ... d4!) would have given him good compensation. As played, White gained both a material and a positional advantage. But again the Champion was let down by his desire to get at the enemy king as soon as possible. In the heat of the struggle he overlooked Black's clever reply 38 ... ♖b1+!, and Karpov left the hall apparently happy with the adjourned position. This game was destined to become the longest played between Kasparov and Karpov.

The Champion conducted the first adjournment session calmly and precisely, winning a pawn and remaining the exchange up. But the resourceful Karpov set up a fortress, which to many experts seemed impregnable. They considered Kasparov's long think before the second adjournment as indicating the absence of a winning plan. But the Champion was engaged in . . . arithmetic, so that the 50 move rule should not operate (if during this time no pawn was moved and no piece taken, the game would be drawn). Thus after 64 g5 White had to win before move 114. When the second sealed move (89 ♖a7) was made, there remained only 25 moves to the draw. The winning path found by Kasparov proved shorter, and on move 102 Karpov resigned.

99

Kasparov-Karpov
Scotch Game

1	e4	0.00	e5	0.02
2	♘f3	0.00	♘c6	0.02
3	d4	0.00	exd4	0.02
4	♘xd4	0.00	♘f6	0.02
5	♘xc6	0.00	bxc6	0.02
6	e5	0.01	♕e7	0.03
7	♕e2	0.01	♘d5	0.03
8	c4	0.01	♘b6	0.04

Karpov avoids 8 ... ♗a6, as he played in Game 14.

Kasparov, on the other hand, was evidently agreeable to a repetition. We would remind you that there Black gained a perfectly good game, although things were very complicated. So what was the point? At the present moment we can only hazard a guess. The first supposition is that on this occasion Karpov did not want a complicated game. The next is that he was afraid of a surprise.

And, perhaps the most likely supposition – during their analysis of Game 14, he and his helpers had discovered an important improvement for White.

The text move is not new, and had already occurred in tournament play.

9　♘d2　*0.12*

In the match bulletin Boris Spassky suggests 9 ♗f4, but now comes the unexpected 9 ... ♕b4+ and White, to avoid losing a pawn (*10 ♕d2 ♘xc4; 10 ♘c3 ♗a6*) is forced to give up the right to castle. Later we discovered the game Jouser-Kiprov, correspondence 1983, where after 9 ... ♕b4+ 10 ♔d1 ♗a6 11 b3 0-0-0 Black gained an advantage.

9	...		♕e6	0.11
10	b3	0.14	a5?!	0.17

An interesting but risky continuation, with the primary idea of establishing the bishop at b4. The drawback to it is that Black loses time and falls behind in development, which will certainly tell in the future.

Here Black has usually played 10 ... ♗e7 11 ♗b2 0-0, which looks sound enough. Bednarski-Gligorić, Havana 1967, continued 12 ♕e4 d5 13 exd6 cxd6 14 ♗d3, while Seeliger-Palciauskas, correspondence 1978, went 12 0-0-0 d5 13 exd6 cxd6 14 ♕f3 d5 15 cxd5 cxd5

16 ♗d3 ♕h6. In both cases Black equalised.

11 ♗b2   0.24   ♗b4   0.33

Black is inconsistent, for which, of course, there are reasons. First 11 ... a4 and only then ... ♗b4 would have been in accordance with the task he had set himself. But after 12 ♕e3 ♗b4 13 ♗d3 (now White is ready to complete his development, castling either short or long, depending on circumstances) Black faces a difficult choice. He has three possibilities:

(a) 13 ... axb3 14 axb3 ♖xa1+ 15 ♗xa1 0-0 16 0-0. Now White is ready for ♘f3, and it is clear that Black's strategy has failed.

(b) 13 ... d5 14 0-0 when, of course, it is dangerous to win a pawn by 14 ... ♗xd2 15 ♕xd2 dxc4 16 bxc4 ♘xc4 17 ♗xc4 ♕xc4 18 ♗a3, but otherwise the white knight goes to f3.

(c) 13 ... d6. Here kingside castling does not work in view of 14 ... a3, when on 15 ♗d4 there follows 15 ... c5. But 14 0-0-0 places Black in a difficult position. Now the idea of ... a3 has to be abandoned, since the bishop retreats to a1, while after 14 ... dxe5 15 ♕xe5 the ending is difficult for Black.

12 a3!?   0.31

Straight away Kasparov forces Black to make up his mind. At the same time he gains the advantage

of the two bishops.

12 ...   ♗xd2+ 0.45
13 ♕xd2   0.33

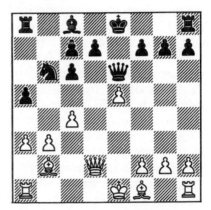

A sharp and interesting position with, apparently, chances for both sides. White has the advantage of the two bishops and prospects of an attack on the kingside. True, he is slightly behind in development. And finally, the arrangement of his queenside pawns gives Black the chance of beginning play on the light squares with ... a4.

Karpov was evidently counting on this possibility, but he saw that after 13 ... a4 14 c5 ♘d5 15 b4 ♗a6 16 ♗xa6 ♖xa6 17 0-0 White was threatening a strong attack with f2-f4. And on Spassky's recommendation in the bulletin of 15 ... f5, with the aim, while still possible, of blocking this advance, there follows 16 ♗c4, answering 16 ... ♗a6 with 17 ♗a2 followed by queenside castling.

13	...	**d5**	*0.54*

This appears to open up the position prematurely. In the same way that Karpov sensibly refrained from 13 ... a4, so too he would have liked to defer this move. After the natural 13 ... 0-0 Black seems to retain various possibilities (... d6, ... d5, ... f6 and even ... ♗a6), with which White would have to reckon. The attempt to block the position by 14 c5 ♘d5 15 ♗c4, which Karpov may have feared, would not succeed, since 15 ... ♗a6 16 0-0 ♖fb8 leads to a position where Black's pressure on the b-file gives him adequate play. But after 14 0-0-0 the threat of the f-pawn's advance places Black in a very difficult situation. On 14 ... ♗a6 there follows 15 f4! (*15 a4* is also possible).

14	cxd5	*0.40*	cxd5	*1.03*

After 14 ... ♕xd5 15 ♕xd5 ♘xd5 the ending is slightly better for White. Even so, Karpov's decision to stay in the middlegame, as we will see, is risky.

15	♖c1	*0.43*	0-0	*1.24*

Now Karpov sacrifices a pawn. In the event of 15 ... c6 16 ♗d3 Black's position would become dangerous, since after 16 ... 0-0 there follows 17 ♕c2, winning a pawn. And if 16 ... ♗b7 then 17 0-0, and it is difficult to find any way of countering the advance of the f-pawn.

16	♖xc7?!	*0.53*

White should probably have been thinking about the development of his kingside and of removing his king from the centre as quickly as possible. 16 ♗d3 was better. In this case Black's best reaction would have been 16 ... a4 (*16 ... f6 17 0-0*) 17 0-0 axb3 18 f4 with a sharp position, where White's initiative would fully compensate for the sacrificed pawn.

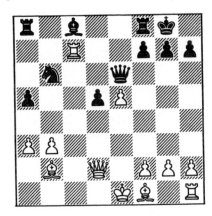

16	...	**♕g6?!**	*1.34*

Karpov would seem to have miscalculated, otherwise he would have made the temporary sacrifice of a second pawn: 16 ... d4!. Exploiting his lead in development, Black opens up the position and obtains active play. White faces a difficult choice. We will examine the following continuations:

(a) 17 ♗xd4 ♖d8 18 ♗e2 ♕xb3 19 ♕b2 (if White wants to keep his extra pawn) 19 ... ♕xb2 20 ♗xb2 ♘d5 21 ♖c2 ♘f4. In the concluding position Black is in no danger.

(b) 17 ♕xd4 ♕xb3 18 ♗e2 (*18 ♗d3 ♗a6!*) 18 ... ♗e6 19 ♖b7! ♖ab8 20 ♖xb8 ♖xb8 21 0-0 ♘c4 or 21 ... ♘a4, and the strong placing of Black's pieces gives him excellent drawing chances.

(c) 17 ♗e2 ♖d8, with good compensation.

(d) 17 ♖c5 ♘d7 18 ♗c4 ♕e7 19 ♖xa5 ♖xa5 20 ♕xa5 ♘xe5 21 0-0 ♘xc4 22 bxc4 ♗b7, with an equal game.

| 17 | f3 | 0.58 | ♗f5?! | 1.35 |

Since Black's position later becomes difficult almost by force, we consider that 17 ... a4 was a better chance, weakening White's hold on c4.

18	g4	1.14	♗b1	1.36
19	♗b5	1.35	♖ac8	1.40
20	♖xc8	1.35	♖xc8	1.40
21	0-0	1.38	h5	1.58
22	h3	1.48	hxg4	2.05
23	hxg4	1.49	♗c2	2.05

Nothing is achieved by 23 ... ♖c2 24 ♕d4 ♕h6 25 ♖f2.

| 24 | ♕d4 | 1.56 |

The threat of e5-e6 forces Black's next move.

| 24 | ... | | ♕e6 | 2.05 |

| 25 | ♖f2 | 1.58 | ♖c7 | 2.08 |

Karpov defends skilfully. This prophylactic move is simply essential. It indirectly protects g7 and also makes possible the manoeuvre ... ♘d7-f8, defending the king. If immediately 25 ... ♘d7 then 26 f4 ♕xg4+ 27 ♖g2 ♕e6 28 ♗xd7 ♕xd7 29 e6 etc.

| 26 | ♖h2 | 2.05 | ♘d7 | 2.14 |

26 ... ♗xb3 is bad in view of 27 ♕d3.

| 27 | b4? | 2.05 |

With this move Kasparov makes it harder for himself to realise his advantage.

From move 17 up to this point the World Champion has played, in our opinion, irreproachably. He was evidently tired of the fact that his extra pawn at b3 was 'hanging', although it was still immune for at least one more move. And he makes what we consider to be an inaccurate move.

27 a4! came into consideration. Apart from the fact that the bishop at b5 is supported, the important a3 square is vacated for the dark-square bishop to be included in the attack. 27 ... ♕b6 is not possible on account of 28 ♗xd7, winning a piece. If 27 ... ♘f8 then 28 ♗a3 with two threats: mate after 29 ♗xf8 and also 29 ♗d6. After 28 ... ♗xb3 (*28 ... ♘g6 29 ♗d6 ♖c8 30 ♗a6 ♖c6 31 ♕a7, or 30 ... ♗xb3 31 ♗xc8 ♕xc8 32 ♕e3*) 29 ♗xf8 ♖c1+ 30 ♔g2 ♖c2+ 31 ♔g3 ♖xh2 32 ♗xg7 White wins.

27	...		axb4	2.14
28	axb4	2.13	♘f8	2.16

Now the play takes on a different character. The exchange of pawns has resulted in the opening of the a-file, which can be used by Black to invade the white position.

29	♗f1	2.14

A further inaccuracy. 29 ♗e2 was better, threatening the advance of the f-pawn. Then things would have been more difficult for Black than in the game.

29	...		♗b3	2.24
30	♗d3	2.20		

Perhaps Kasparov should have moderated his appetite. His chances would be improved in the endgame. His king is very exposed,

and to build up an attack on the enemy king is very difficult, especially in view of his lack of time on the clock. 30 f4 was already possible, and if 30 ... ♕xg4+ 31 ♖g2 ♕d1 32 f5. White threatens e5-e6, and in the event of the exchange of queens he has a clear advantage in the ending. But that would not have been Kasparov!

31	...		♗c4	2.25
31	♗f5	2.20		

The alternative was 31 ♗b1 ♕a6 32 ♕d2 ♗a2 33 b5 ♕a4 34 b6 ♖b7, when Black retains chances of saving the game.

31	...		♕e7	2.26
32	♕d2	2.20	♖c6	2.26

A good prophylactic move.

33	♗d4	2.20	♖a6	2.26

The play has become extremely sharp. Now Kasparov's king is also in danger.

34	♗b1	2.21	♖a3	2.26
35	♖h3	2.25	♖b3	2.27
36	♗c2	2.25	♕xb4	2.28
37	♕f2	2.25		

(see diagram)

37	...		♘g6	2.28

Black has regained his pawn, but now he has to parry mating threats. At the moment ♕h4 is threatened. The tempting 37 ...

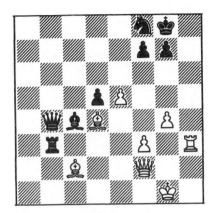

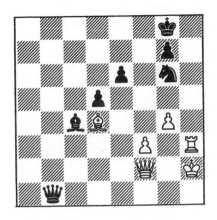

♘e6 does not work in view of 38 ♕h4 ♔f8 39 ♗xb3, when 39 ... ♕xb3? loses immediately to 40 ♗c5+ and mate next move, while if 39 ... ♗xb3 40 ♗f2.

38   e6?   *2.26*

After literally walking a tightrope during the last few moves, combining defence with the threat of a mating attack, with this impulsive move Kasparov simply gives up a pawn and allows his opponent saving chances. He should have simply played 38 ♗xb3, when the realisation of his material advantage would have been only a question of time.

38	...	♖b1+	*2.28*
39	♗xb1	*2.27*	♕xb1+	*2.29*
40	♔h2	*2.28*	fxe6	*2.29*

Here the game was adjourned and Kasparov sealed his 41st move.

41   ♕b2   *2.41*

As we see, after sensible reflection Kasparov himself forces the exchange of queens. The resulting ending favours White. He is the attacking side, and therefore in the given instance, although it is an endgame, the presence of opposite-colour bishops is to his advantage. Of course, the realisation of this advantage involves great difficulties. The experts gave White roughly a forty per cent chance of winning.

| 41 | ... | ♕xb2+ | *2.29* |
| 42 | ♗xb2 | *2.41* | ♘f4 | *2.29* |

Black defers the advance ... e5, in order to hinder the rook from coming into play. In passing, he sets a little trap – on 43 ♖g3 there follows 43 ... ♗e2, and it is not clear how the rook can be brought out.

| 43 | ♖h4 | *2.42* | ♘d3 | *2.29* |

44	♗c3	2.42	e5	2.34
45	♔g3	2.46	d4	2.39
46	♗d2	2.46	♗d5	2.43
47	♖h5	2.48		

Preventing 47 ... ♘b2 followed by ... ♘c4. If the knight should reach c4, Black's pieces will be well coordinated and the advance of the d-pawn will be well supported.

47	...		♔f7	3.01
48	♗a5	2.51	♔e6	3.05
49	♖h8	2.57	♘b2	3.11
50	♖e8+	3.00	♔d6	3.11

50 ... ♔f6 loses a pawn after 51 ♗d8+.

51	♗b4+	3.06	♔c6	3.11
52	♖c8+	3.06		

If 52 ♖xe5 ♘d3.

52	...		♔d7	3.11
53	♖c5	3.06	♔e6	3.11
54	♖c7	3.06	g6	3.26
55	♖e7+	3.06	♔f6	3.26
56	♖d7	3.22		

White has achieved some success by driving the bishop from d5 and not allowing Black to set up the formation ♗d5/♘c4, which would give him counterchances.

56	...		♗a2	3.26
57	♖a7	3.44	♗c4	3.42

If 57 ... ♗d5 then 58 ♗e7+ ♔e6 59 ♗g5. Now 59 ... ♘c4 followed by the advance of the d-pawn does not work. White plays 60 ♖g7 d3

61 ♖xg6+ ♔d7 62 ♖a6 d2 63 ♖a1 e4 64 fxe4 ♗xe4 65 ♗xd2, or 61 ... ♔f7 62 ♖f6+ ♔g7 63 ♖a6 d2 64 ♗xd2 ♘xd2 65 ♖d6 ♘f1+ 66 ♔f2 ♗c4 67 ♖d1 ♘h2 68 ♔g2, and wins.

58	♗a5	4.06	♗d3	3.49

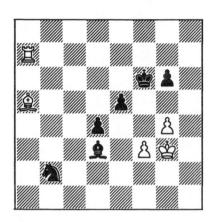

59	f4!	4.08

Here is Kasparov's main plan – by exchanging his f-pawn for the e-pawn he brings his king into play.

59	...		exf4+	3.54
60	♔xf4	4.09	♗c2	3.55
61	♖a6+	4.09	♔f7	3.57
62	♔e5	4.14	♘d3+	4.10

If 62 ... d3 then 63 ♖a7+ ♔e8 64 ♔e6.

63	♔xd4	4.14	♘f2	4.11
64	g5	4.14		

In this position Karpov recommended 64 ♖c6, destroying the

coordination of the black pieces. Black has only one move: 64 ... ♗a4 (otherwise he loses a piece) 65 ♖c7+ ♚e6 66 g5, when the knight cannot return to its own territory.

64	...		♗f5	*4.12*
65	♗d2	*4.16*	♚e7	*4.12*
66	♚d5	*4.17*	♘e4	*4.16*
67	♖a7+	*4.18*	♚e8	*4.17*
68	♗e3	*4.18*	♘c3+	*4.18*
69	♚e5	*4.18*	♚d8	*4.18*
70	♗b6+	*4.18*	♚e8	*4.18*
71	♖c7	*4.21*	♘e4	*4.18*
72	♗e3	*4.21*	♘g3	*4.24*
73	♗f4	*4.30*	♘h5	*4.29*

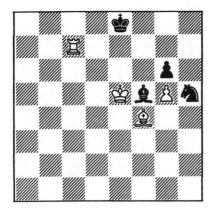

Black has set up a fortress, but at a high price: his king is cut off on the back rank, and as soon as his knight is stalemated at h5 the white king will gain the opportunity to penetrate into enemy territory. Hence White's plan is to (1) place his bishop at e5; (2) take his king to d8, and (3) transfer his king to e7.

74	♖a7	*4.35*	♚f8	*4.30*
75	♗h2	*4.41*	♘g7	*4.31*
76	♗g1	*4.42*	♘h5	*4.31*
77	♗c5+	*4.42*	♚g8	*4.33*
78	♚d6	*4.54*	♚f8	*4.34*
79	♗d4	*4.55*	♗g4	*4.35*
80	♗e5	*5.13*		

The first part of the plan has been carried out. The second part is technically more difficult. Up to move 88 Kasparov is unable to find a way of achieving his aim. Therefore there is no point in us following his actions. Rather the opposite: we can observe how Karpov hinders the opponent's actions.

80	...		♗f5	*4.30*
81	♖h7	*5.14*	♚g8	*4.38*
82	♖c7	*5.14*	♚f8	*4.41*
83	♚c6	*5.16*	♚g8	*4.45*
84	♖e7	*5.20*	♚f8	*4.48*
85	♗d6	*5.22*	♚g8	*4.50*
86	♖e8+	*5.22*	♚f7	*4.50*
87	♖e7+	*5.24*	♚g8	*4.50*
88	♗e5	*5.25*	♚f8	*4.51*

In this position the game was adjourned for the second time. Kasparov sealed his move early (the time remaining in the session being added to his clock) so as to try and solve the problem at home with the help of his team, and possibly a computer. Moreover, his task was complicated by the

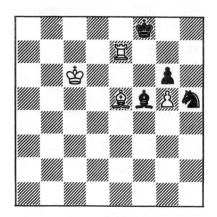

50-move rule coming into operation, so that he had to find a win
within 26 moves.

On the resumption Kasparov
played very purposefully. We will
draw your attention to the key
moments.

89	♖a7	6.19	♗g4	4.58
90	♔d6	6.19	♗h3	5.10
91	♖a3	6.19	♗g4	5.10

Things are not changed by 91 ...
♔f7 92 ♔c7 ♔e6 93 ♗d6 ♔d5 94
♖e3, when White's king penetrates
to h6 and he then wins by sacrificing the exchange at g6.

92	♖e3	6.19	♗f5	5.25
93	♔c7	6.19	♔f7	5.31
94	♔d8	6.20		

The second part of the plan is

carried out.

94	...		♗g4	5.32
95	♗b2	6.20	♗e6	5.36

95 ... ♘f4 loses to 96 ♖e7+ ♔f8
97 ♗a3 ♔g8 98 ♖e4.

96	♗c3	6.20	♗f5	5.37
97	♖e7+	6.20	♔f8	5.38
98	♗e5	6.21	♗d3	5.40
99	♖a7	6.21	♗e4	5.42
100	♖c7	6.22		

So as later to have c8 for a rook
check.

100	...		♗b1	5.42
101	♗d6+	6.22	♔g8	5.54
102	♔e7	6.23		

The third part of the plan is
carried out. **Black resigns**, since
on 102 ... ♘g7 there would have
followed 103 ♖c8+ ♔h7 104 ♗e5.

GAME SEVENTEEN   5 December

Before the 17th game Karpov was expected to take a postponement, but this did not happen. The Ex-World Champion arrived for the game wearing a new suit, aiming for immediate revenge. He undoubtedly wanted to win one back, but he did not try desperately to do this, and played as though nothing had happened. It seemed that this was not the most difficult Grünfeld for Black, and Kasparov succeeded in equalising without any great problems. Lulled by the peaceable course of the game, everyone was expecting a shortened working day. Kasparov too relaxed. He did not want to go in for a continuation where White acquired an isolated passed pawn in the centre, and preferred passive defence. But the seemingly harmless position proved to be rather dangerous. One inexact move, one lost tempo (21 ... 罝e8?) turned into a great misfortune for Black. White seized control of the only open file, his pieces took up dominating positions, whereas the black pieces were pressed back inside their own territory. White's dark-square bishop got through an impressive amount of work. Its route of c1-e3-g5-d2-c3-a5-c7-f4-d2 was not only spectacular but also effective. As usual Karpov ran short of time. Kasparov's position was hopeless, and it was only because of this factor that he made the last few moves. As soon as the time control was reached, he immediately congratulated the opponent on his victory.

Karpov-Kasparov
Grünfeld Defence

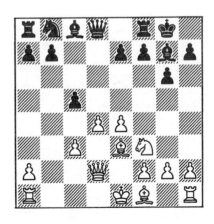

1	d4	0.05	♘f6	0.00
2	c4	0.05	g6	0.00
3	♘c3	0.05	d5	0.00
4	cxd5	0.05	♘xd5	0.00
5	e4	0.05	♘xc3	0.00
6	bxc3	0.00	♗g7	0.00
7	♗e3	0.05	c5	0.01
8	♕d2	0.07	0-0	0.02
9	♘f3	0.07		

9   ...   ♗g4   0.02

Kasparov deviates from 9 ... ♕a5, as played in Game 15, where, as we know, he obtained a slightly inferior ending.

10   ♘g5!?   0.20

What is the point of this unexpected sortie? Obviously White does not want his kingside pawns to be spoiled. On the other hand, the normal reaction 10 ♗e2 cxd4 11 cxd4 ♘c6 12 ♖d1 leads to a theoretical position which is considered equal, and not without reason (after *12 ... ♗xf3 13 ♗xf3 e5 14 d5 ♘d4* or *14 dxe5 ♘xe5*).

10 ♘e5, with the same idea, is an interesting alternative. But after 10 ... cxd4 11 cxd4 ♗xe5 12 dxe5 ♕xd2+ 13 ♗xd2 ♘c6, despite White's two bishops, Black's lead in development assures him of at least an equal game.

10   ...   cxd4   0.29
11   cxd4   0.21

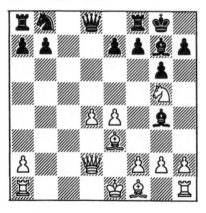

11   ...   ♘c6   0.29

This move makes 9 ... ♗g4 pointless.

11 ... h6 is of undoubted interest. Let us first give some general considerations. Black played 9 ... ♗g4 in order to put pressure on d4, and he was prepared to exchange his bishop for the white knight. Therefore we consider that, in this sense, 11 ... h6 was the consistent continuation. Of course, the situation has changed somewhat – after 12 h3 (*12 ♘xf7* is an interesting idea, but one from the realms of fantasy) 12 ... hxg5 13 hxg4 the g5 pawn is en prise, which naturally gives cause for alarm. But Black has gained an even greater lead in development over his opponent. Here we suggest a plan by which he very quickly deploys all his forces and obtains a good game: 13 ... ♕d7! (*13 ... ♘c6* is weaker, in our opinion, since after *14 ♖d1 ♕d7 15 ♗e2* it is difficult for Black to increase the pressure) 14 ♗e2 ♖d8 15 ♖d1 ♕a4!. This is the point of the manoeuvre begun with 13 ... ♕d7: the queen is moved to a4, where it occupies a very strong position, and only then is the knight developed. After 16 f3 (White has to defend his e4 pawn, in order to be able to advance *d4-d5*) Black has a choice between 16 ... ♘a6 followed by 16 ... ♖ac8, and even 16 ... ♘c6 17 d5 ♖ac8.

12	h3	*0.22*	♗d7	*0.30*
13	♖b1	*0.27*		

A favourite Karpov motif, which has already occurred several times in this match. Both here and in earlier games the idea is to try and provoke ... b6. But by tactical means Kasparov renders this move superfluous, and therefore the natural 13 ♘f3 would have been better.

13	...		♖c8!	*0.47*
14	♘f3	*0.39*		

Not 14 ♖xb7 ♘xd4 15 ♗xd4 ♗xd4 16 ♕xd4 ♖c1+ 17 ♔d2 ♖d1+ 18 ♔xd1 ♗a4+, when Black wins.

14	...		♘a5	*0.54*
15	♗d3	*0.51*	♗e6	*0.59*
16	0-0	*0.52*		

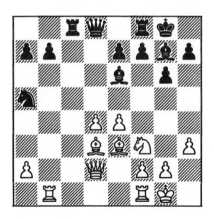

Karpov has finally completed his development, and here we can take stock. White has maintained his strong pawn centre, and this gives him an advantage. On the other hand, Black is ready to occupy c4, which reduces this advantage to the minimum.

16	...		♗c4	*1.00*

16 ... ♘c4 would seem to be worse, since after 17 ♗xc4 ♗xc4 18 ♖fc1 the bishop at c4 is rather awkwardly placed.

17	♖fd1	*1.01*	b5	*1.21*

Reinforcing his control of c4 is Black's only sensible continuation.

18	♗g5	*1.16*	a6	*1.32*
19	♖bc1	*1.25*	♗xd3	*1.34*
20	♖xc8	*1.33*	♕xc8	*1.34*
21	♕xd3	*1.33*	♖e8?	*1.49*

An illogical move. All the same the queen has to move to b7, and therefore it would have been better to do this immediately. Now Black ends up in a difficult position.

22	♖c1	*1.36*	♕b7	*1.50*
23	d5	*1.43*	♘c4	*1.51*

(see diagram)

24	♘d2!	*1.43*

By exchanging the black knight White invades on the open c-file and gains a decisive advantage.

24	...		♘xd2	*2.04*

Black's position is only slightly easier after 24 ... h6 25 ♗h4 g5 26 ♗g3 ♘xd2 27 ♖c7, or 27 ♕xd2

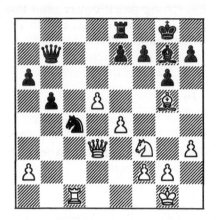

罩c8 28 罩xc8+ ♛xc8 29 e5, with a great advantage.

25 ♗xd2! *1.54*

After 25 ♛xd2 b4 Black would have gained a little air.

25 ... 罩c8 *2.05*

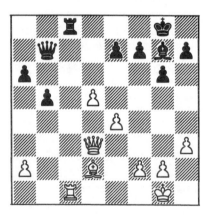

26 罩c6! *2.02*

Strategically the game is decided, and now the tactical execution commences.

26 ... ♗e5 *2.05*

Of course, 26 ... 罩xc6 27 dxc6 ♛xc6 28 ♛d8+ leads to mate.

27	♗c3!	2.09	♗b8	2.07
28	♛d4	2.16	f6	2.10
29	♗a5	2.16	♗d6	2.14
30	♛c3	2.20	罩e8	2.15

A further gain – now White has also secured control of the c-file. The outcome of the game is not in doubt.

31	a3	2.20	♔g7	2.17
32	g3	2.22	♗e5	2.18
33	♛c5	2.23	h5	2.21
34	♗c7	2.24	♗a1	2.21
35	♗f4	2.24	♛d7	2.21
36	罩c7	2.24	♛d8	2.21
37	d6	2.26		

In the end it is White's main trump that has the last word.

37	...		g5	2.22
38	d7	2.26	罩f8	2.22
39	♗d2	2.26	♗e5	2.23
40	罩b7	2.27		

Now that the time control has been reached, **Black resigns** in this hopeless position.

GAME EIGHTEEN   8/9 December

In the previous game Kasparov had allowed Karpov to exact immediate revenge for his defeat in the 16th game. Now Karpov himself ended up in a similar situation. Evidently the burden of positive emotions is not easy to bear.

But Karpov began the game at an exceptionally rapid tempo. This was a demonstration of his confidence in himself, and in the variation of the Ruy Lopez with a pawn sacrifice chosen by him. It has to be said that Karpov convinced the experts in the press centre: they quickly appreciated that for the pawn Black had obvious compensation. The times on the two clocks – 16 minutes for Karpov and an hour more for Kasparov – intensified this impression. But after 21 ♕c4!, not considered by anyone but found by the Champion at the board, everything changed. When Karpov thought over his reply for 1 hour 3 minutes (a record for this match), it became clear that in his thorough analysis beforehand this move had not been considered! Three moves later he missed a good opportunity (23 ... ♖b6!), and the evaluation of the position changed sharply. White retained his extra pawn and the superior position.

That evening the strongest grandmasters in the world, who had gathered in Lyon for a meeting of the GMA directors, were guests in the press centre. After a press conference Timman, Short, Ljubojević, Larsen and Kavalek crowded round the monitor. Their opinion was unanimous: "White has a won position".

The game was adjourned. Kasparov still had a chance to spoil everything if he had sealed an apparently strong knight move (suggested by many experts), which would in fact have thrown away the win. But the World Champion found the genuinely strongest continuation, won the game on resumption, and again took the lead.

Afterwards the players 'as usual' exchanged opinions on the game. "Yes, ♕c4 – that was the move!" Karpov admitted. It is a good thing when intransigent opponents can acknowledge the mastery of each other!

113

Kasparov-Karpov
Ruy Lopez

1	e4	0.00	e5	0.01
2	♘f3	0.00	♞c6	0.01
3	♗b5	0.00	a6	0.01
4	♗a4	0.00	♞f6	0.01
5	0-0	0.00	♝e7	0.01
6	♖e1	0.00	b5	0.01
7	♗b3	0.01	d6	0.02
8	c3	0.01	0-0	0.02
9	h3	0.01	♞d7	0.03
10	d4	0.02	♝f6	0.03
11	a4	0.04	♝b7	0.04
12	♘a3	0.05	exd4	0.05
13	cxd4	0.05		

Up till now this is a repetition of the 12th game, played in New York. We refer the reader to our comments on that game.

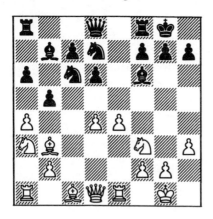

13	...	♞b6	0.08

Is this stronger than 13 ... ♞a5 14 ♗a2 b4 15 ♘c4 ♞xc4 16 ♗xc4, as Karpov played in New York?

14 ♗f4! *0.51*

White decides to give up his Spanish bishop since, with some justification, he fears 14 axb5 axb5 15 ♗f4 b4. If now 16 ♘c4 then 16 ... ♖xa1 17 ♕xa1 ♞xc4 18 ♗xc4 ♞xd4. On 16 ♘c2 there follows 16 ... ♞a5 17 ♞xb4 ♞xb3, when Black regains his pawn. That only leaves 16 ♘b5, but then comes 16 ... ♗a6.

14	...	bxa4	0.11
15	♗xa4	0.52	♞xa4	0.11
16	♕xa4	0.52		

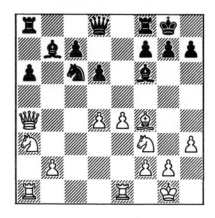

Let us take stock. White has a good centre and an associated spatial advantage. All his pieces have promising posts. Perhaps Black's only achievement is that he has exchanged White's light-square bishop, so that he has the advantage of the two bishops. There can be only one conclusion

– Karpov's opening innovation has not justified itself, and he faces a difficult defence.

16	...	a5	*0.12*

This is Black's only hope – to establish his knight at b4.

17	♗d2	*0.57*	♖e8	*0.13*
18	d5	*1.02*	♘b4	*0.14*

If 18 ... ♘e5 19 ♘xe5 ♗xe5 20 ♘c4, with a positional advantage for White. Karpov sacrifices a pawn to exchange White's second bishop. This seems to us the best defence. Now Black's dark-square bishop becomes very strong.

19	♗xb4	*1.09*	axb4	*0.15*
20	♕xb4	*1.09*	♖b8	*0.16*
21	♕c4	*1.18*		

On 21 ♕d2 Black would have freed his second bishop by 21 ... c6.

Here Karpov thought for a long time. He was concerned not so much by being a pawn down as by the absence of any counterplay. Regaining the pawn by 21 ... ♗xb2 22 ♖a2 ♗f6 23 ♘b5 ♕d7 24 ♘fd4 does nothing to ease Black's position. Karpov carries out an interesting plan: he brings out his bishop to a6, after which the black bishops rake the entire board.

21	...	♕c8!?	*1.19*
22	♘d4	*1.32*	♗a6	*1.20*
23	♕c3	*1.32*		

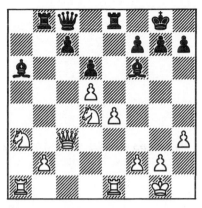

23	...	c5?	*1.23*

There was not yet any necessity to go in for variations involving the exchange of one of the bishops, especially the dark-square one. 23 ... ♖b6! came into consideration, with the idea of building up pressure on the b-file and preparing ... c6 or ... c5 in a more favourable situation, it being very important to retain the dark-square bishop. In the possible variation 24 ♘ac2 ♕b7 25 b3 ♗b5 26 ♕d2 c5 27 dxc6 ♗xc6 it would be far from simple for Kasparov to realise his material advantage.

24	dxc6	*1.33*	♗xd4	*1.23*
25	♕xd4	*1.33*	♕xc6	*1.23*
26	b4!	*1.41*		

Possibly it was this move that Karpov underestimated when he embarked on the exchanging operation. The advance of this pawn restricts Black's play. Now White completely dominates the position.

26	...	h6	1.29
27	♖e3	1.42	♖e6	1.41
28	f3	1.45	♖c8	1.46
29	♖b3	1.48	♗b5	1.58
30	♖b2	1.51	♕b7	2.00
31	♘c2	1.54	♕e7	2.03
32	♕f2	2.03		

It is hard to understand why it was necessary to withdraw the queen from its strong position. In our opinion, the logical 32 ♘e3 would have concluded the game within a few moves. Instead Kasparov gives the opponent an opportunity to complicate matters.

32	...	♖g6	2.05
33	♘e3	2.14	♕e5	2.07
34	♖bb1	2.14	♗d7	2.10
35	♖a5	2.17	♕e7?	2.13

Black sounds the retreat, although he had nothing to lose by going forward. He should have played 35 ... ♕d4 36 ♖d5 ♕a7 or 36 ... ♕b6, when he could still have resisted.

36	♖a7	2.20	♕d8	2.14
37	♘d5	2.21	♔h7	2.14
38	♔h2	2.23	♖b8	2.15
39	f4	2.24	♖e6	2.15
40	♕d4	2.26	♕e8	2.16

White is a pawn up with the better position, and therefore the win is simply a matter of time and technique.

Kasparov sealed his 41st move.

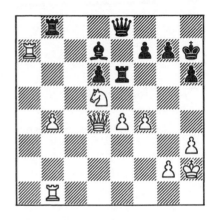

41	♖e1	2.29

41 ♘c7 ♖xe4 42 ♕d3 does not win the exchange in view of 42 ... ♗b5.

41	...	♗c6	2.17
42	♕d3	2.30	♕f8	2.19
43	♖c1	2.50	♗xd5	2.20
44	exd5+	2.50	♖g6	2.21
45	♕f5	2.52	♔g8	2.23
46	♖ac7	2.52	♖f6	2.23
47	♕d7	2.52	♖d8	2.28
48	♕xd8	2.52		

The simplest.

48	...	♕xd8	2.28
49	♖c8	2.53	♕f8	2.29
50	♖1c4	2.53	♖f5	2.31
51	♖xf8+	2.54	♔xf8	2.31
52	♖d4	2.54	h5	2.32
53	b5	2.56	♔e7	2.33
54	b6	2.56	♔d7	2.33
55	g4	2.56	hxg4	2.34
56	hxg4	2.56	♖f6	2.34
57	♖c4	2.56	**Resigns**	

GAME NINETEEN   *12 December*

When a King's Indian set-up was reached on the board, Kasparov's former trainer Iosif Dorfman, who had helped him in previous matches but was now working in France, doubtfully shook his head. "Good openings shouldn't be changed. The loss in Game 17 bore no relation to the opening."

But chess fans filling the *Palais des Congrès* that day did not regret that Kasparov had chosen this double-edged opening as Black. A complicated strategic struggle developed, full of inner tension. It was only on move 21 that the first exchange of pawns occurred, and only on move 32 – the first exchange of pieces. The play was most unusual. Thus White, after avoiding 'normal' castling, then nevertheless evacuated his king to its usual position 'on foot' on moves 28-30: ♔e1-f1-g1-h1! Not surprisingly, during the game the experts' evaluation of the position changed diametrically several times. But when, just before the time control, Black opened up the position on the queenside at the cost of a pawn and developed strong piece pressure, their opinion was that Black had a decisive attack.

And suddenly, a move before the time control, the monitor showed the two players in conversation. And when they began signing their scoresheets, it became clear that the game had finished. But with what result? "Karpov has resigned" someone suggested. It soon transpired that Kasparov had offered a draw, and it had been accepted. This news caused confusion. Winning variations for Black poured forth in profusion.

"But did you consider such a variation as fatigue?" Kasparov asked after the game.

The position was sharp, Black was a pawn down, and his previous move had not been the best. In view of this, and also the match situation, Kasparov had decided not to take a risk.

Karpov-Kasparov
King's Indian Defence

1	d4	0.00	♘f6	0.00
2	c4	0.00	g6	0.00
3	♘c3	0.00	♗g7	0.00

Kasparov's reversion to the King's Indian Defence after his defeat in Game 17 may indicate that he is aiming for more complicated play. In our opinion, the positions which have arisen in the Grünfeld Defence are more in Karpov's style.

4	e4	0.00	d6	0.00
5	♘f3	0.00	0-0	0.00
6	♗e2	0.02	e5	0.01
7	♗e3	0.04	c6	0.01

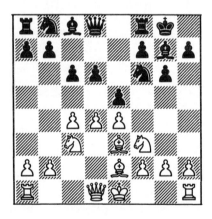

We should straight away mention that this is the first time in the match that Black's last move has occurred. It will be remembered that the 11th game went 7 ... exd4 8 ♘xd4 ♖e8 9 f3 c6 10 ♕d2 d5 11

exd5 cxd5 12 c5 ♖xe3. But instead of 10 ♕d2 there is also the recommendation by theory that White should play 10 ♗f2, not allowing the exchange sacrifice (compare our comments to the aforementioned game). Now Karpov's reaction to the move order chosen by Black becomes understandable. For our part, we must conclude that both players consider the exchange sacrifice to be correct.

| 8 | d5 | 0.14 | | |

By closing the centre the Ex-World Champion takes the play along different strategic lines, occurring for the first time in the match.

| 8 | ... | | ♘g4 | 0.04 |

A seemingly natural, but highly dubious reaction. The dividends from this manoeuvre are small, whereas its drawbacks are obvious. All variations with ... cxd5 are now ruled out, since White recaptures on d5 with his knight. And sooner or later Black will be forced to play ... c5. One of the main continuations in this position used to be considered 8 ... cxd5 9 cxd5 ♘e8 10 ♘d2 f5 11 ♘c4 (*11 f3 is weaker on account of 11 ... ♗h6*).

| 9 | ♗g5 | 0.14 | f6 | 0.04 |
| 10 | ♗h4 | 0.15 | ♘a6 | 0.05 |

This is said to be a new continuation and, to judge by the commentary in the match bulletin, the older 10 ... c5 was better. As evidence the game Wirthensohn-Watson, Thessaloniki 1988 (0-1) is given. Without wishing to enter into a discussion, we should mention that after 10 ... c5 White could have sharply changed plan – 11 0-0 h5 12 ♘e1 ♘h6 13 h3 ♘f7 14 ♘d3 ♗h6 15 ♗g3, when he is ready to meet ... f5 with f2-f4.

11 ♘d2 *0.20*

Routine play, although quite appropriate here. The alternative was 11 0-0, when White plays similarly to the above variation.

11	...	♘h6	*0.12*
12	a3 *0.29*	♘f7	*0.14*
13	f3 *0.31*	♗h6	*0.18*
14	♗f2 *0.35*		

After preventing 14 ... ♗e3 White is now ready to castle.

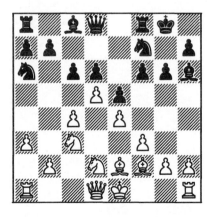

Here we can take stock. White

has a clear spatial advantage. He controls more space and is ready to begin an offensive on the queen-side. Black, on the other hand, must stick to waiting tactics, since his offensive on the kingside holds no promise of success – the opponent's king is not there (compare the commentary to Game 3).

14 ... f5 *0.20*

It is significant that this normally aggressive thrust has only defensive functions here. Now ... ♕g5 is a possible threat.

15	♕c2 *0.46*	♗d7 *0.35*
16	b4 *0.58*	c5 *0.36*
17	♖b1 *0.59*	b6 *0.50*

Black has parried the immediate threats on the queenside, but for the moment that is the end of his success.

18 ♘f1 *1.07* **♗f4?!** *1.15*

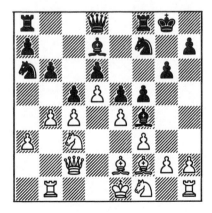

A futile waste of time, and

besides, the bishop is badly placed at f4. But Kasparov is trying to provoke an advance of the kingside pawns. The main danger for Black is an attack on the f5 pawn. 18 ... ♕f6 was preferable, a prophylactic move that simultaneously connects his rooks.

19	g3?	1.19

The start of an incorrect plan which unnecessarily weakens the white position on the kingside. The bishop at f4 should have been disregarded. After 19 ♗d3 Black would have been in difficulties, for example 19 ...♘h6 20 ♘g3 followed by castling.

19	...		♗h6	1.17
20	h4	1.19	♘c7	1.20
21	g4	1.36	fxg4	1.22
22	fxg4	1.36	♗f4	1.22

As we see, the bishop has returned to f4, from where it can never now be driven away.

23	♘e3	1.37	♘e8	1.26
24	♘cd1!	1.42		

Of this last series of moves (beginning with the 19th), this is the first one of any substance. It met with the approval of the experts. Now White's minor pieces are coordinated and they ensure the solidity of his position on the kingside.

24	...		h6	1.48

Kasparov, realising that he will be unable to open up the game on the kingside, deprives Karpov of the same possibility.

25	h5	1.53	g5	1.49

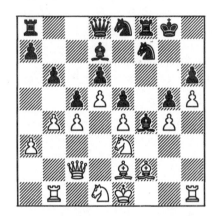

A new and original situation, which is not easy to evaluate. Each side has his pluses, and even the dark-square bishop at f4, which occupies a strong position, may in certain situations be only the equivalent of a pawn.

26	♖g1	2.00

We do not wish to suggest any different ideas, but will assume that the plan chosen by Karpov is correct. Indeed, White needs to remove his king from the centre and defend his g4 pawn when the necessity arises. We will now ask the reader to note the number of moves it takes the Ex-World Champion to solve this problem.

We see that, beginning with 26 ♖g1, this takes exactly five moves. Now let us try doing this more quickly. Let us play 26 0-0 ♘f6 27 ♔h1 ♕c8 28 ♖g1 – only three moves. It now becomes clear why Kasparov is the first to begin play on the queenside. At this point, in the analogous position, his knight is already at b7. And another small detail can be added: as will soon be apparent, the rook would be better placed at g1 than at g2.

26	...		♘f6	*1.49*
27	♖g2	*2.04*	♕c8	*1.51*
28	♔f1	*2.07*	♘d8	*1.52*
29	♔g1	*2.10*	♘b7	*1.53*
30	♔h1	*2.16*		

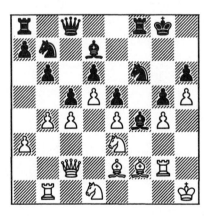

30	...		cxb4	*1.55*

And so, Kasparov begins active play on the queenside. White's minor pieces and also his king's rook are shut off from the scene of action. The situation changes sharply in favour of Black.

31	axb4	*2.17*	a5	*1.55*
32	♘f5	*2.18*		

White cannot join battle on the queenside as long as his g4 pawn is attacked.

32	...		♗xf5	*1.56*
33	exf5	*2.18*	axb4	*2.03*
34	♖xb4	*2.20*	♘c5!	*2.03*

Kasparov correctly sacrifices a pawn. If 34 ... ♘xd5?! then 35 ♖b5 ♖a5 36 ♕b1, when White regains his pawn and his pieces become active.

35	♖xb6	*2.21*	♘ce4	*2.04*
36	♖c6	*2.22*	♕b7	*2.08*
37	♗e1?	*2.24*		

A serious mistake, although understandable. Seriously short of time, Karpov instinctively withdraws his bishop to a supposedly better square. But in doing so he leaves the opponent with his two knights, which are a powerful attacking force. In addition he overloads his back rank, along which an invasion presents a great danger. Better was 37 ♗d3 (or perhaps even *37 c5*) 37 ... ♘xf2+ 38 ♘xf2 ♖a1+ 39 ♖g1 ♖fa8 (*39 ... ♖xg1+ 40 ♔xg1 ♗e3 41 ♔g2* and White has good defensive resources) 40 ♖xa1 ♖xa1+ 41 ♔g2, and White defends successfully. Now Black acquires serious winning chances.

| 37 | ... | | ♖a1 | 2.11 |
| 38 | ♗f3 | 2.25 | ♘c5 | 2.13 |

This allows White a respite, which, as it turns out, saves him. Since White can hardly contemplate taking the knight, there was no reason to withdraw it. After 38 ... ♖b8 there would have been no defence against the invasion of the black pieces. For example, 39 ♗xe4 ♘xe4 40 ♕xe4 ♖xd1 41 f6 ♖xe1+! (*41... ♕b1 42 ♕g6+ with drawing chances*) 42 ♕xe1 ♕b3, with decisive threats.

| 39 | ♗c3 | 2.25 | ♖c1 | 2.19 |

After playing 39 ... ♖c1 Kasparov offered a **draw**, which was immediately accepted. It is fairly obvious that this offer was, to say the least, premature. We have

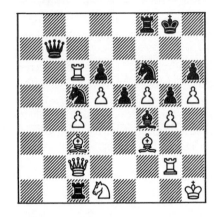

analysed this position a great deal, but have been unable to find any explanation for what happened. Possibly Kasparov saw something that frightened him. Therefore it seems to us that he himself is better placed to give an answer.

GAME TWENTY   15 December

In this encounter Karpov 'reprieved' the Zaitsev Variation of the Ruy Lopez, which had been removed from his repertoire after the memorable and highly eventful 4th game. The approaching finish and the unfavourable match situation forced the Ex-World Champion to seek complications in every game, irrespective of the colour of the pieces.

For 17 moves the two players were resolutely 'in agreement'. It was clear that both were aiming for one and the same position. The only thing not clear was who was the hunter, and who was the quarry! Karpov was apparently the first to 'shoot'. It is possible that the natural 18 ... ♘f6 had not occurred previously. But note the times on the clocks. Kasparov replied almost instantly – 19 ♗h2!. His 'shot', it would appear, was better aimed: Karpov's search for a reply took about half an hour. It has to be assumed that the theoretical duel was won by the World Champion. Grandmaster Lyev Polugayevsky, who a few moves earlier had expressed confidence in Black's position, now unreservedly admitted that White had an enduring advantage.

The position abounded in tactical possibilities, and everyone in the press centre, making all kinds of sacrifices (it is easier to give up someone else's pieces!), began attacking the shaky defences of the black king. True, no one was able to find a forced variation. But the storm factor – the ratio of the attacking and defending forces – was so great that no one was in any doubt: there must be a way to win! And the World Champion showed how it should be done. During the course of a lengthy combination he sacrificed in turn a bishop, knight and queen, and then, almost as in draughts (chequers), he immediately regained the material with interest.

In contrast to the 4th game, here Kasparov's brilliantly conducted attack received its logical conclusion.

The German grandmaster Wolfgang Unzicker exclaimed: "About this game alone one could write a whole book!"

Kasparov-Karpov
Ruy Lopez

1	e4	0.00	e5	0.05
2	♘f3	0.00	♘c6	0.05
3	♗b5	0.00	a6	0.06
4	♗a4	0.00	♘f6	0.06
5	0-0	0.00	♗e7	0.06
6	♖e1	0.01	b5	0.06
7	♗b3	0.01	d6	0.07
8	c3	0.01	0-0	0.07
9	h3	0.01	♗b7	0.07

Returning to the Zaitsev Variation. It can be assumed that the match situation will force Karpov to go in for sharp play even as Black.

10	d4	0.01	♖e8	0.07
11	♘bd2	0.02	♗f8	0.08
12	a4	0.02	h6	0.09
13	♗c2	0.02	exd4	0.10
14	cxd4	0.02	♘b4	0.10
15	♗b1	0.04	c5	0.10
16	d5	0.04	♘d7	0.10
17	♖a3	0.06	f5	0.10

Indeed, our suppositions are proved correct. Karpov chooses the ultra-sharp but very risky variation which occurred in New York in the 4th game of the match.

18 ♖ae3 0.10

This idea was employed by Timman against Karpov in their Final Candidates Match (Kuala Lumpur 1990). The idea of it is clear enough. White transfers his second rook to the centre and

hopes, in the event of the possible ... fxe4, to exploit the potential accumulated by him on the kingside. It will be remembered that in the 4th game Kasparov played 18 exf5.

18 ... ♘f6 0.14

In the aforementioned game against Timman, Karpov abandoned the undermining of White's centre and chose the cautious but less active 18 ... f4 19 ♖3e2?! (*19 ♖a3!*) 19 ... ♘e5, with a good position for Black. He did not risk opening the b1-h7 diagonal, even with the win of a pawn. Indeed, after 18 ...fxe4 19 ♘xe4 ♘xd5 (*19 ... ♗xd5 20 ♗d2*) 20 ♖3e2 ♘7f6 21 ♘xf6+ ♘xf6 22 ♖xe8 ♘xe8 23 ♘h2 ♘f6 24 ♘g4 White has a strong attack.

19 ♘h2 0.11

In anticipation of the position opening up, Kasparov prepares ♘g4. At the same time, for the moment he himself does not want to take on f5, which would block the b1-a7 diagonal.

19 ... ♔h8 0.37

The unusual duel continues.

20	b3	0.34	bxa4	0.57
21	bxa4	0.37	c4	0.57

In order to have the possibility of blocking the light-square bishop's diagonal by ... ♘d3. As before

21 ... fxe4 22 ♘xe4 gives White a strong attack, for example: (a) 22 ... ♘fxd5 23 ♖g3 ♘f6 (♗xh6 was threatened) 24 ♘xf6 ♕xf6 25 ♗d2 ♕d4 26 ♘g4; (b) 22 ... ♘bxd5 23 ♘xf6 ♖xe3 24 ♖xe3 ♘xf6 25 ♗b2; (c) 22 ... ♗xd5 23 ♘xf6 ♖xe3 24 ♖xe3 ♕xf6 25 ♗d2 ♕d4 26 ♘f3.

22 ♗b2 *0.53*

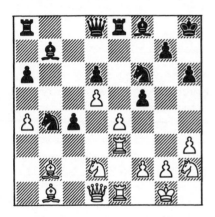

White sticks clearly to his policy. He moves his dark-square bishop to an attacking position and simultaneously completes the mobilisation of all his forces. The tension on the board has increased almost to the limit.

22 ... fxe4 *1.31*

Here Karpov loses his nerve and deviates from the strategic course that the two players have been following over the last few moves. Now the diagonal for White's Spanish bishop is opened.

In our opinion, 22 ... ♖c8 was at the least consistent, and this move also completes Black's development. After this White would have faced the difficult problem of how to force Black to capture on e4. He can try to do this by 23 ♕f3 or 23 ♖f3, or he can defer it for one move after 23 ♗c3 a5 (*23 ... ♘d3 24 ♗xd3 cxd3 25 ♗xf6 ♕xf6 26 ♖xd3* is insufficient for Black). Let us examine these possibilities:

(a) 23 ♕f3 ♕d7, and little is achieved by 24 ♗xf6 gxf6, when the c4 pawn becomes dangerous.

(b) 23 ♖f3 fxe4 24 ♘xe4 ♘xe4 25 ♖xe4 (or *25 ♗xe4 ♖xe4 26 ♖xe4 ♗xd5*) 25 ... ♗xd5 26 ♖xe8 ♕xe8 27 ♕d2 ♘d3 28 ♖e3 ♕xa4, with an unclear game.

(c) The inclusion of 23 ♗c3 a5 is no advantage to White. The only difference is that now the black knight is defended.

23 ♘xe4 *1.02* **♘fxd5** *1.40*
24 ♖g3 *1.16* **♖e6** *1.54*

An essential defensive move.

25 ♘g4 *1.35* **♕e8?** *2.11*

White has a very strong attack, which is practically impossible to parry. 25 ... ♘d3 was rather more tenacious, although after 26 ♗xd3 cxd3 27 ♕d2 ♕e8 28 ♔h2 (*28 ... ♖xe4? 29 ♕xh6+ ♔g8 30 ♗xg7!*) or 27 ... ♕e7 28 ♔h2 White still has a great advantage.

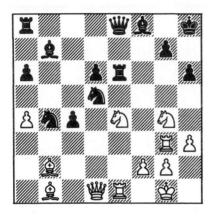

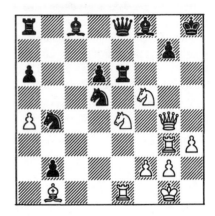

26 ♘xh6! *1.40*   **c3**   *2.15*

In the event of 26 ... ♖xh6 various ways of conducting the attack are possible. We will offer the reader one of these, which we consider the prettiest. Several grandmasters, including ourselves, and led by the young Soviet grandmaster Igor Glek, examined the following: 27 ♘g5 ♕h5 28 ♔h2 c3 (*28 ... ♕xd1 29 ♘f7+ ♔g8 30 ♘xh6+ ♔h8 31 ♖xd1 c3 32 ♗xc3 ♘xc3 33 ♖xc3 gxh6 34 ♖c7 ♗c8 35 ♖e1 ♘d5 36 ♖f7 ♔g8 37 ♗a2 etc*) 29 ♖e6! ♔g8 (*29 ... ♕xd1 30 ♖xh6+ gxh6 31 ♘f7 mate*) 30 ♖xh6 ♕xh6 31 ♕f3 and White wins.

27 ♘f5   *1.42*   **cxb2**   *2.23*
28 ♕g4   *1.42*   **♗c8**   *2.24*

Black is a piece up and his b-pawn has penetrated to the second rank, but White's attacking poten-

tial is so great that a defence is practically impossible. However, in the match bulletin Jon Speelman states that Black's move was a mistake, and that it may have been better to defend with 28 ... g6. Karpov played 28 ... ♗c8 and lost virtually by force, and therefore we can agree with the English grandmaster that other possibilities were at any event no worse. But as regards 28 ... g6, we cannot agree that it was any better, since after the prophylactic move 29 ♔h2 (after all, ... gxf5 is not a threat) Black's position cannot be successfully defended.

29 ♕h4+   *1.42*   **♖h6**   *2.24*

After 29 ... ♔g8 30 ♔h2 there is no defence.

30 ♘xh6   *1.42*   **gxh6**   *2.25*
31 ♔h2   *1.55*   **♕e5**   *2.25*

Black is not saved by 31 ... ♖a7

32 ♘f6 ♕f7 33 ♖e8 ♘xf6 (*33 ...*
♕xf6 34 ♕xf6+ ♘xf6 35 ♖xf8+)
34 ♕xh6+ ♘h7 35 ♕xh7+ ♕xh7
36 ♖xf8+.

32   ♘g5   *1.55*

The concluding attack is straight-
forward but elegant.

32	...		♕f6	2.27
33	♖e8	1.56	♗f5	2.27

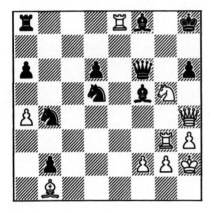

34   ♕xh6+ *1.57*

Here the curtain could have
been lowered, but Karpov, in
time trouble, automatically keeps
moving until the control is reached.
34 ♘f7+ ♕xf7 (*34 ... ♔h7 35 ♕xf6*)
35 ♕xh6+ ♗h7 36 ♖xa8 is
equally crushing.

34	...		♕xh6	2.27
35	♘f7+	1.57	♔h7	2.27
36	♗xf5+	1.57	♕g6	2.27
37	♗xg6+	1.57		

White begins 'bringing in the
harvest', but 37 ♖xg6 would have
concluded the game more elegant-
ly, when there is no satisfactory
defence against the mate.

37	...		♔g7	2.27
38	♖xa8	1.58	♗e7	2.28
39	♖b8	1.58	a5	2.28
40	♗e4+	1.58	♔xf7	2.28
41	♗xd5+	1.58	**Resigns**	

GAME TWENTY-ONE   19/20 December

Kasparov's choice of opening showed that he was not intending to sit it out in passive defence, but was prepared in an open battle to try and gain the one point he needed to retain his title of Champion. In the psychological sense this was the correct thing to do. The closeness of his goal and the postponement claimed (after his previous win) could have had a weakening effect on him, and Karpov is not one to forgive such an error.

As in the first game of the match, Karpov chose the Sämisch Variation, which, to judge by the Champion's expression, came as a surprise to him. After brief reflection he chose a variation which is a kind of hybrid of two defensive systems. The players castled on opposite sides, but did not rush into action, preferring strategic manoeuvring. It was only in the fifth hour of play that the position sharpened. Both sides succeeded in approaching directly the enemy king, Black having to give up a pawn to do this. The last few moves of both players were made with their flags hanging.

At the adjournment Karpov, after thinking for nearly half an hour, sealed the strongest move. But the resumption showed that, despite a great amount of work, it was the Kasparov team that had coped better with the analysis of the adjourned position. It transpired that the plan of defence, involving an attack on White's kingside pawns, was a surprise to Karpov. He was unable to create the most difficult problems for Black, and the position soon became drawish. The outcome of the game became clear, but the adjournment session still continued for a long time. However, Karpov can hardly be condemned for trying to exploit every practical chance.

After the game the spectators were rewarded by the chance of observing a joint analysis of the adjourned position, which Kasparov and Karpov conducted on the stage. For half an hour, variations which had remained 'off-stage' flashed by on the screens. Chess fans saw for themselves how complex the endgame labyrinth was, and what an enormous amount of analytical work had been done by both players during the adjournment.

Karpov-Kasparov
King's Indian Defence

1	d4	0.00	♘f6	0.00
2	c4	0.00	g6	0.00
3	♘c3	0.00	♗g7	0.00
4	e4	0.00	d6	0.00
5	f3	0.00		

The situation in the match gave this game a particular character. For the last time but one Karpov was playing White, and only a win would leave him with hopes of a favourable outcome. At this important moment he chooses the Sämisch Variation against the King's Indian Defence, which, it will be remembered, he employed in the first game of the match – an interval of twenty games. An association involuntarily suggests itself with the novel of the famous French writer Alexandre Dumas *Twenty Years After*. (If one game is compared with a year of life, which is a quite permissible comparison.)

5	...		0-0	0.05
6	♗e3	0.01	e5	0.05

Kasparov has a wealth of experience and a great knowledge of the King's Indian Defence, which gives him the opportunity to vary; therefore there is no reason to think that 6 ... c6 is worse than the old variation begun by the text move. Here the explanation is more probably of a purely psycho-logical nature. The World Champion simply wanted to take his opponent away from a variation which had evidently been specially prepared for this game.

7	d5	0.03		

This leads to a closed game.

7	...		♘h5	0.05
8	♕d2	0.04	f5	0.05
9	0-0-0	0.10		

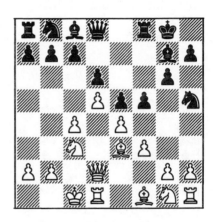

In this variation White has to castle long, since the preparation of kingside castling would take a great deal of time.

9	...		a6!?	0.06

It is curious that one of the authors of the book employed this move forty years ago. The idea of it is to put pressure on e4 with the help of the flank blow ... b5, for example 10 ♘ge2 b5 11 c5 b4 12 ♘a4 fxe4.

10 ♗d3   0.22

Of course, this move is by no means bad, but forty years ago 10 ♔b1 was considered more accurate, and only after 10 ... ♘d7 – 11 ♗d3.

10 ...   c5   0.09
11 dxc6?! 0.30

This non-King's Indian move undoubtedly eases Black's position. From the viewpoint of theory, 11 exf5 gxf5 12 ♘ge2 is preferable in such positions, planning a later g2-g4.

11 ...   ♘xc6   0.10

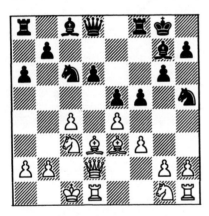

We have on the board a new situation. The game has opened up. Black has gained the opportunity of easily developing his pieces, and the weakness of his d6 pawn, especially taking account of White's queenside castling, is illusory. For example, 12 ♗e2

♗e6 13 b3 b5 14 ♕xd6 ♕e8 15 ♘d5 ♖f7 16 ♘c7 ♖xc7 17 ♕xc7 ♖c8, and the white king is in danger.

12 ♘d5   0.35

We see that Karpov aims in the first instance to prevent a future ... b5.

12 ...   ♗e6   0.24
13 ♗b6   0.41

The task set himself by Karpov is fulfilled.

13 ...   ♕d7   0.24
14 ♘e2   0.45   ♖ac8   0.34
15 ♔b1   0.47   ♕f7   0.35
16 ♖he1   0.53

From Karpov's preceding actions it is not clear why he made this move. We may be incorrect and he did in fact have some plan, but we were unable to see it, and he was most probably acting according to the method of the great player and theorist of the 1920s and 1930s Aron Nimzowitsch, who stated: "If you do not know what to do, centralise" (the pieces, of course).

16 ...   ♔h8   0.48

Kasparov evidently considers it useful to remove his king from the a2-g8 diagonal. This is indeed a useful prophylactic move.

17 ♗c2   1.15

This move, opening the d-file for the heavy pieces, creates certain threats. Black now has to reckon with the capture on f5 followed by ♘e3. Out of curiosity we should point out that Karpov thought over this move for 22 minutes.

17 ...   ♘f6!   *0.57*

Kasparov realises that the storm clouds are gathering over his position, and he takes suitable measures, one of which is to drive the bishop from b6 by ... ♘d7.

18   ♗d3   *1.24*

A courageous decision. The Challenger required only 9 minutes to realise that the plan of 18 exf5 gxf5 19 ♘g3 would not achieve its aim in view of 19 ... ♘d7 20 ♗f2 b5!, when the advantage passes to Black.

18	...	♘d7	*1.01*
19	♗g1	*1.25*	♘c5	*1.05*
20	♘b6	*1.28*	♖cd8	*1.25*
21	♘c3	*1.33*		

Much as he dislikes it, White is forced to relinquish his control over d4, but in return he firmly seizes the d5 square.

21	...	♘d4	*1.32*
22	♘cd5	*1.34*	♗xd5	*1.37*
23	♘xd5	*1.39*	fxe4	*1.39*
24	fxe4	*1.45*		

Evaluating this position, it seems to us that Black has a certain advantage. This is based on the fact that White has a bad bishop at d3, which can only carry out defensive functions and is itself a target for attack.

24   ...   b5?   *1.39*

It is clear to us that this seemingly active move is premature, and merely creates a weak pawn at b5. We think that, even if only temporarily, Black should have seized control of the f-file, an aim which is pursued by 24 ... ♕d7. After the essential 25 h3 (not allowing the queen to go to g4) there follows 25 ... ♖f7 26 ♖f1 ♖df8. Black's advantage increases and it is far from simple for White to defend.

25	♖f1	*1.52*	♕d7	*1.42*
26	cxb5	*1.54*	axb5	*1.43*
27	♖xf8+?	*1.58*		

It is not clear why Karpov concedes the f-file, and then begins trying to win it back. The immediate 27 h3 was more accurate. Now, however, the initiative is again with Black.

27	...	♖xf8	*1.45*
28	h3	*1.59*	♕d8	*1.52*
29	♗xd4	*2.11*		

The threat of 29 ... ♕h4 forces White to give up his bishop.

29   ...   exd4   *1.52*

The position has changed, and we think that Black has somewhat

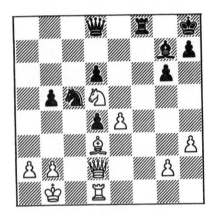

improved his chances, since he has gained the opportunity to develop play on the dark squares.

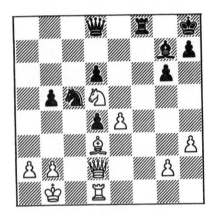

30   ♕e2   2.12

White's first problem is to neutralise the action of the black rook on the f-file, and so Karpov prepares ♖f1.

30   ...   ♕h4?!   2.11

If Kasparov was playing for a win, and we think that this was the case, then this move is a mistake. After White's reply it transpires that Black can play on only at the cost of worsening his position. Therefore to us 30 ... ♕g5!? seems more interesting. Now White cannot play 31 ♖f1, in view of 31 ... ♖xf1+ 32 ♕xf1 ♕d2, when Black wins. In addition, 31 ... ♕g3 is threatened. The only move to parry this threat is 31 ♘b4, defending the bishop at d3 (*31*

♗xb5 is bad, of course, if only because of *31 ... d3 32 ♗xd3 ♘a4*) 31 ... ♕e3 32 ♖f1 ♖c8 (*31 ... ♖e8* is also good) 33 a3 (the attempt to drive away the queen by *33 ♖f3* ends in mate after 33 ... *♕c1+! 34 ♔xc1 ♘b3++*) 33 ... ♘b3. The black pieces occupy dominating positions and it is not at all easy for White to defend.

31   ♖f1!   2.13   ♖e8   2.16

We do not know whether Kasparov was playing for a win at this point. But after 31 ... ♖xf1+ 32 ♕xf1, neither 32 ... ♘xd3 33 ♕xd3 ♕e1+ 34 ♔c2 ♕f2+ 35 ♔b3 (after *35 ♕d2 d3+ 36 ♔xd3 ♕d4+ 37 ♔e2 ♕xe4+ 38 ♘e3* the game would probably end in a draw) 35 ... ♕xg2 36 ♘c7!, nor 32 ... ♘xe4 33 ♕e2 ♘f6 34 ♘xf6 ♗xf6 35 ♗xb5 guarantees him safety.

Reverting to the variation given in the previous note with 30 ... ♕g5, only now in an inferior version since an important tempo has been lost, would nevertheless have guaranteed Kasparov a draw: 32 ... ♕g3 33 ♘b4 (*33 ♔c2 ♘xd3 34 ♕xd3 ♕xg2+ 35 ♔b3 h5*, and compared with the similar variation given above Black has an extra tempo) 33 ... ♕e3 34 ♕e2 (*34 a3 ♘xe4*) 34 ... ♕g1+.

After the text move the black pieces are forced to retreat, and the initiative passes to White.

32	♖f4	*2.16*	♕g5	*2.16*
33	a3	*2.21*	h5	*2.21*
34	♔a2	*2.26*	b4!?	*2.26*

Fearing that White will fully consolidate his position, after which the b5 pawn will fall, Kasparov sacrifices a pawn to provoke a fresh wave of complications.

35	axb4	*2.26*	♖a8+	*2.26*
36	♔b1	*2.26*	♘b3	*2.26*
37	♔c2	*2.27*	♘a1+	*2.26*
38	♔b1	*2.27*	♘b3	*2.26*
39	♕f2	*2.28*	♕d8	*2.28*
40	♖f7	*2.29*	♕e8	*2.29*

Here the game was adjourned and Karpov sealed his 41st move. This position provoked much interest and discussion. Its evaluation was clear – White had a definite advantage. But was it sufficient? Much depended on the sealed move.

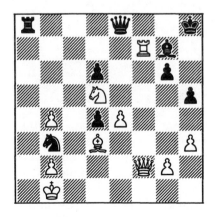

When the envelope was opened it transpired that Karpov had sealed:

41	b5!	*2.56*

On this rather surprising move, which removes the attack on c5, to where the black knight can now safely return, Karpov spent 27 minutes. The aim of it is to cut off the black queen from a4.

We, of course, do not know what other possibilities Karpov considered and rejected when he was sealing. At any event, it can be said that, during what was most probably a sleepless night before the resumption, the Ex-World Champion and his team analysed only this continuation. The problem for Kasparov and his team was a much broader one. They were also obliged to spend considerable time and effort on other possibilities for White. We also do not know which continuations Kasparov's group considered the most dangerous.

We, for our part, also carried out some analytical work. Apart from the text move, the authors considered, among others, three main continuations as being the most dangerous for Black:

(a) 41 ♘e7. Here we fairly quickly established that after 41 ... ♖a1+ 42 ♔c2 ♘c5! (with the threat of ... *♕a4+*) 43 ♘xg6+ ♔h7 44 ♘f8+ ♔h8! (*44 ... ♔g8 45 ♖xg7+ ♔xg7 46 ♕xd4+* clearly favours White) White is forced to give perpetual check.

(b) 41 ♘b6. This rather shrewd move, covering the a4 square, presents a serious danger to Black. The best defence is probably 41 ... ♖a1+ (if *41 ... ♖b8 42 ♘d7 ♖b7 43 ♘e5!*) 42 ♔c2 ♘c1! 43 ♖xg7 ♘xd3 44 ♕xd4 ♕c6+ 45 ♘c4 ♘e5 (*45... ♕a4+? 46 ♔xd3 ♕b3+ 47 ♔e2*) 46 ♖xg6 ♕xc4+ 47 ♕xc4 ♘xc4. White has three pawns for a knight, and although things are by no means simple, the chances are on his side.

(c) Only a draw is given by the exchange sacrifice 41 ♖xg7 ♔xg7 42 ♕f6+ ♔h7 43 ♕g5 ♕c6 44 ♘f6+ ♔g7 45 ♘xh5+ ♔h7.

41	...	♖a1+	2.30
42	♔c2 2.56	♘c5	2.30

The only defence.

43	♖xg7 2.56	♔xg7	2.30
44	♕xd4+ 2.56	♕e5	2.30
45	♕xe5+ 2.56	dxe5	2.30

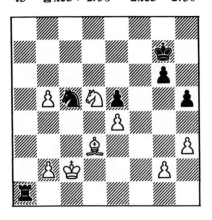

This ending has arisen by force. For the exchange White has two pawns, and although they are doubled, the pawn at b5 constitutes a powerful force.

46 b6! *2.56*

Now Black does not have time to bring his king to the queenside, and he must act very precisely. He must without fail pick up the g2 pawn, in order to create counter-chances on the kingside.

46	...			♖g1	2.30
47	♘e3	2.57		♖e1	2.30
48	♘c4	3.02		♖g1	2.30
49	♘e3	3.05		♖e1	2.31

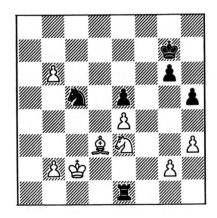

Here Karpov was obviously trying to decide when to play b2-b4, whether with his knight at e3 or c4. He decided on the latter, at the time when his g2 pawn was attacked, and Kasparov immediately gave up his knight for the b6 pawn.

The question arises, would it not have been better to advance the b-pawn now? Let us consider this continuation: 50 b4. In this case Black has only one move: 50 ... ♘d7 51 ♘c4 ♖g1 52 b7 ♖xg2+ 53 ♔c3. If now 53 ... ♔f6, then 54 ♘b6 ♘b8 55 ♗b5 ♔e7 56 ♘d7 ♔d6 57 ♘xb8 ♔c7 58 ♘d7 ♔xb7. The analysis can be continued, but it is clear that at the least White has serious winning chances. If instead 53 ... ♖g3, then 54 ♘xe5 ♘b8 55 b5, again with good winning chances.

50	♘c4	3.31	♖g1	2.59
51	b4	3.26	♖xg2+	2.59
52	♔c3	3.26	♘a4+	2.59

As we see, Kasparov does not play his knight to d7, which would lead to a position examined above, but sacrifices his knight immediately.

53	♔b3	3.26	♘xb6	2.59
54	♘xb6	3.26	♖g3	3.00
55	♔c3?!	3.26		

A rather strange move. We do not understand why White did not play 55 ♔c4, simultaneously breaking the pin. After 55 ... ♖xh3 56 ♘d7 ♖f3 57 b5 he would have had good winning chances.

55	...		♖xh3	3.00
56	b5	3.29	h4	3:01

57	♘c4	3.44	♖xd3+!	3.02

Here we lost interest in analysing any further. White loses his last pawn and the draw becomes obvious.

58	♔xd3	3.44	h3	3.02
59	b6	3.44	h2	3.02
60	b7	3.44	h1=♕	3.02
61	b8=♕	3.44	♕f1+	3.02
62	♔c3	3.45	♕c1+	3.02
63	♔b3	3.48	♕d1+	3.02
64	♔a2	3.51	♕a4+	3.02
65	♘a3	3.51	♕xe4	3.02
66	♕c7+	3.52	♔h6	3.05
67	♘c4	3.54	♕d5	3.08
68	♔b2	3.54	e4	3.20
69	♕f4+	3.56	♔g7	3.22
70	♔c3	4.05	♕d3+	3.29
71	♔b4	4.05	♕d4	3.29
72	♕h4	4.05	♔f7	3.46
73	♔b5	4.25	♕d5+	3.50
74	♔b4	4.25	♕d4	3.50
75	♕h7+	4.27	♕g7	3.50
76	♕h1	4.27	♕d4	3.50
77	♕h4	4.28	♔g8	3.57
78	♕f4	4.57	♔g7	3.58
79	♕c1	4.59	♔f6	4.22
80	♔b5	5.03	♕d5+	4.24
81	♔b4		♕d4	
82	♔b5		♕d5+	
83	♔b6		♕d4+	
84	♔c6		♔e6	
85	♘e3		♕a4+	
86	♔b6	5.14	♕b4+	4.28

Draw agreed, on Kasparov's proposal.

GAME TWENTY-TWO   26 December

It was in different moods that the two players embarked on their 22nd game, with different tasks facing them. With a lead of two points, Kasparov that day would be quite happy with a draw, which would prolong his Champion's authority for a further three years. The appearance in the press centre of his entire training team (for the first time in the match) emphasized the importance of the occasion and their confidence in its favourable outcome. In the three remaining games Karpov was obliged to play for only one result – a win. And although in the 1986 match he happened to win three successive games against Kasparov, few believed that such a repetition was possible.

Once again the Zaitsev Variation. It would appear that Karpov had no other opening that would lead to a complicated game. Or perhaps the week's break preceding this game had helped him to find some new possibilities. Kasparov had no intention of 'asking' for a draw, but accepted the challenge. He was even ready to repeat the 4th game, perhaps the sharpest of the match. But Karpov introduced a correction: he captured the d5 pawn a move earlier. Kasparov was still hoping for a transposition of moves, but Black had other plans. At the cost of two pawns Karpov gained a threatening initiative. After 25 ... ♘c5 Kasparov's trainers began to look anxious. But when the World Champion carried out a 'relieving' operation, by giving up a piece for the far-advanced black pawn in the centre, they markedly calmed down, assessing the position as drawish. Spassky even thought that White, with three pawns for a knight, had the more promising position. Indeed, after the exchange of light-square bishops Kasparov had more chances of attack than Karpov. 39 b6! would have set Black difficult problems. But Kasparov had already seen a perpetual check which would retain his title, and without much thought he forced it. Sweeping away the cordons set up by the arbiters, journalists rushed onto the stage to obtain from the Champion the first immediate interviews.

Kasparov's new victory was greeted with applause by the spectators.

Kasparov-Karpov
Ruy Lopez

1	e4	0.00	e5	0.09
2	♘f3	0.00	♘c6	0.09
3	♗b5	0.01	a6	0.09
4	♗a4	0.01	♘f6	0.10
5	0-0	0.01	♗e7	0.10
6	♖e1	0.01	b5	0.10
7	♗b3	0.01	d6	0.10
8	c3	0.01	0-0	0.11
9	h3	0.01	♗b7	0.11
10	d4	0.02	♖e8	0.11
11	♘bd2	0.02	♗f8	0.13
12	a4	0.02	h6	0.13
13	♗c2	0.02	exd4	0.13
14	cxd4	0.03	♘b4	0.14
15	♗b1	0.03	c5	0.14
16	d5	0.03	♘d7	0.14
17	♖a3	0.05	f5	0.15

This is the third time in the match that we have seen this position (cf. also Games 4 and 20). As we have already mentioned in our commentary to Game 20, the match situation again forces Karpov to employ this sharp and risky variation. Of course, it was obvious that the Ex-World Champion had prepared some improvement.

18   exf5   *0.06*

As in Game 4, Kasparov chooses the most critical continuation.

18   ...   ♗xd5   *0.18*

An innovation. Although in the present game it justified itself, it is as yet too early to judge to what extent it changes the evaluation of the position, compared with the usual 18 ... ♘f6. Black's plan is obvious – to transfer his bishop to f7 for the defence of his king and to support his actions in the centre and on the queenside. However, as we have indicated earlier, the insecure position of the black king may tell at any moment.

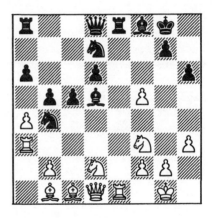

19   ♘e4   *0.10*

This routine move helps Black to implement his plan. Possibly Kasparov simply committed a transposition of moves. He could have tried to exploit the new situation on the board in other ways, one of which was 19 axb5. Now 19 ... axb5 20 ♘e4 leads to the position for which Kasparov was aiming. Therefore 19 ... ♖xe1+

is the only move, and after 20 ♕xe1 axb5 White has the possibility, exploiting the absence of the knight from f6, of obtaining the better game by 21 ♗e4 (*21 ♕e2 is also good, when any defence of the b5 pawn disrupts Black's plans*) 21 ... ♘f6 22 ♗xd5+ ♘bxd5 23 ♕e6+ ♔h7 24 ♘e4 ♘xe4 (*24 ... ♖xa3? 25 ♘g5+!*) 25 ♖xa8 ♕xa8 26 ♕xe4 ♘b6 27 ♕c2, and the poor position of the black king gives White the advantage.

19   ...   ♗f7   0.21

Karpov has carried out his plan. Black seizes the initiative and threatens ... d5.

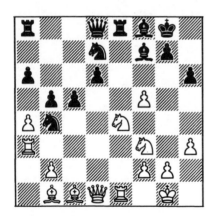

20   axb5   0.35

Kasparov thought over this move for 25 minutes. Possibly he was considering variations such as 20 ♗g5. If the sacrifice is accepted White obtains attacking chances, but 20 ... ♕b6 casts doubts on this sortie.

20   ...   d5   0.21

20 ... axb5 can be met by 21 ♘xd6.

21   ♘c3   0.35   ♖xe1+   0.25
22   ♘xe1 0.42

No better is 22 ♕xe1 d4, with play similar to that in the game.

22   ...   d4   0.59
23   ♘a2   0.49

Forced, otherwise Black's attack develops with material equal.

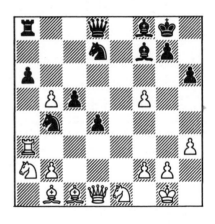

23   ...   ♘xa2   1.14

In our opinion 23 ... a5 was stronger, leading to more complicated play. In this case Black would have avoided the exchange of rooks, since after 24 ♘xb4 axb4 25 ♖xa8 ♕xa8 the position is clearly in his favour – the pawn mass on the queenside gives him excellent prospects.

24 ♗xa2 0.49 c4 1.15

There is no other way of shutting the light-square bishop out of the game.

25 ♖xa6 0.51 ♘c5 1.16
26 ♖xa8 0.51 ♕xa8 1.16
27 ♗b1 0.57 d3 1.19

The attempt to regain one of the pawns by 27 ... ♕a1 would have allowed White dangerous counterplay after 28 ♗f4 ♕xb2 29 ♗e5.

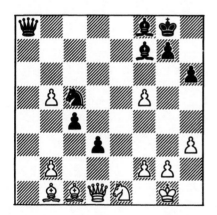

Black appears to have achieved a great deal. He has stalemated White's light-square bishop and intends to regain one of his pawns, after which his advantage will be undisputed. But this impression is deceptive. White, who at the moment is two pawns up, has the possibility of escaping from the blockade by means of a piece sacrifice.

28 ♗e3 1.06 ♕a5 1.23
29 b3! 1.23 ♘xb3 1.27
30 ♘xd3 1.23 cxd3 1.28
31 ♗xd3 1.23

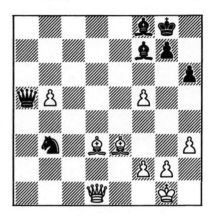

As a result of Kasparov's operation he has three pawns for the piece, his pieces have become active, and since, in the event of the exchange of queens, the endgame is in his favour, his chances are preferable. Black must play very carefully.

31 ... ♘c5 1.46

Black is obliged to keep an eye on the passed b-pawn, and he seizes the opportunity to drive the white bishop to a position from where it cannot take part in a possible attack.

32 ♗f1 1.26 ♕c7 1.51
33 ♕g4 1.37

At last the poor position of the black king, which we have mentioned more than once, begins to tell.

33	...	♔h7	*1.59*

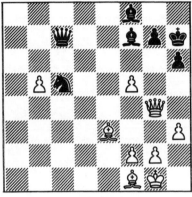

34	♗c4	*1.43*

White exchanges the light-square bishops, after which the weakness of the light squares in the opponent's position is felt. Black cannot avoid the exchange, since on 34 ... ♗e8 there follows 35 ♗xh6!, winning.

34	...	♗xc4	*2.13*
35	♕xc4	*1.45*	♕e5	*2.14*

36	♕f7	*1.50*	♗d6	*2.22*
37	g3	*1.50*	♕e7	*2.25*
38	♕g6+	*2.01*	♔h8	*2.25*

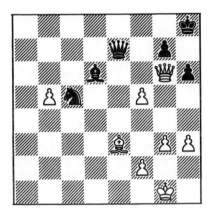

39	♗d4	*2.02*

White has a clear advantage, and after 39 b6 it would have been very difficult for Black to defend. But Kasparov decides to force a draw, thus retaining his title of World Champion.

39	...	♗e5	*2.26*
40	♗xc5	*2.02*	♕xc5	*2.26*
41	♕e8+	*2.02*	♔h7	
42	♕g6+	*2.02*	♔h8	*2.31*
43	♕e8+	*2.03*	**Draw agreed**	

GAME TWENTY-THREE   29 December

The Champion is known, the match continues. But this is no longer a contest for the chess crown. The fate of the money prize is to be decided, and in this match it is a record – three million dollars. In the event of the match being drawn, the prize will be divided equally between the participants. So that this continuation of the match cannot be called a formality!

It was another matter that, having achieved his main aim and still being in a festive mood, Kasparov was hardly prepared psychologically to play at full strength that evening. Although, he was fully aware of the competitive character of his 'perpetual' opponent, his fighting qualities, and his determination to battle to the end. He was aware, and he realised that there would be no easy life for him at the finish.

With his choice of opening Kasparov as though urged himself to engage in a complicated, active game. But the corresponding mood, eager for a fight, was lacking. And the variation itself chosen by Black, positionally dubious, was clearly not in accordance with the match situation. It would have been appropriate, had Black been aiming for complications, and White the opposite – for caution. But Karpov already had absolutely nothing to lose, and he played actively, which was the best solution to the problems in the resulting position. He found a very clear-cut offensive plan and carried it out masterfully. On move 29 Kasparov admitted defeat.

In 1985 Karpov published a book *Miniatures from the World Champions*, which included victories by the champions achieved in not more than 30 moves. In a second edition he would probably be happy to include this game. But the shortest win in games between these two players was achieved by Kasparov on move 25. This occurred in the 11th game of the 1985 match, when Kasparov first won the title of Champion.

	Karpov-Kasparov		2	c4		g6
	King's Indian Defence		3	♘c3		♗g7
			4	e4		d6
1	d4	♘f6	0.01	5	f3	0.01

In the last games of the match, playing White, the Ex-World Champion firmly places his choice on the Sämisch Variation. Although the main question had already been decided – Kasparov had retained his title for a further three years – there was still the little matter of the prize money to be decided. By choosing this continuation, Karpov as though says: "Our duel is not yet over, and I want to find out everything about you!"

5	...		0-0	0.06
6	♗e3		e5	
7	d5	0.02	♘h5	0.08
8	♕d2		♕h4+	

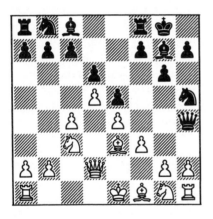

This idea of this clever, but insufficiently correct discovery belongs to David Bronstein. Normally Black sacrifices his queen for two bishops (the dark-square bishop being especially important) and two pawns. This idea was first employed (with the slight difference that, instead of *5 ... 0-0*, Black played *5 ... e5 6 d5 ♘h5 7 ♗e3 ♘a6*) in the game Spassky-Bronstein, Amsterdam 1956.

| 9 | g3 | 0.06 | ♕e7 |

The usual continuation is 9 ... ♘xg3 10 ♕f2 ♘xf1 11 ♕xh4 ♘xe3 12 ♔e2 ♘xc4, but by 13 ♖c1 ♘a6 14 ♘d1 ♘b6 15 ♘h3 ♗d7 16 ♘e3 f6 17 ♖hg1 White gained the advantage in the game Karpov-Velimirović, Skopje 1976. Possibly Kasparov does not agree with this evaluation. It will be remembered that he sacrificed his queen for similar compensation in Game 3. But the World Champion, confident of victory in the match, evidently does not wish to disclose his secrets.

For example, in Spycher-Piket, Groningen 1986-87, Black improved on the above game with 17 ... ♖ae8 (Velimirović's *17... ♖ad8* placed the rook on a tactically vulnerable square), while Kasparov-Seirawan, Barcelona 1989, saw the World Champion playing this variation with White: 17 ♘f2 ♘c8!, with a draw after a complicated battle.

At the same time, the point of this last operation by Kasparov is not easy to understand. Black has played 9 ... ♕e7, a non-essential move, and has provoked g2-g3, which is a useful move for White.

The only point to be discerned in Black's idea is a slight weakening of the f3 square.

10   0-0-0 *0.14*   **f5**
11   exf5! *0.18*

This exchange would seem to disrupt Kasparov's plan. Otherwise, because of his weakness at f3, it is difficult for White to develop his king's knight.

11   ...   **gxf5**
12   ♘h3

Black's unfortunate manoeuvre begins to tell. Had the pawn been at g2, he could have achieved certain gains by 12 ... f4 13 ♗f2 ♗xh3 14 gxh3 ♗f6 15 ♕e1 ♘d7. 12 ♘h3 is an innovation; White prepares g3-g4. Vyzhmanavin-Akopian, Lvov 1990, went 12 ♗d3 a5?! (better *12 ... ♘d7* with the standard idea of *... ♘df6* and the constant threat of *... e4*) 13 ♘ge2 ♘a6 14 f4! with advantage to White.

12   ...   **♘a6**   *0.22*

From here for a long time the knight cannot join the play that develops on the opposite wing. But Black's position is already difficult, and it is not easy to suggest anything better. White's plan is simple – to advance g3-g4, and the pawn sacrifice 12 ... ♗d7 13 g4 fxg4 14 fxg4 ♘f4 15 ♘xf4 exf4 16 ♗xf4 does not give Black

sufficient compensation. 12 ... f4 (with the idea of *13 gxf4 ♗xh3 14 ♗xh3 ♘xf4*) is also unsatisfactory on account of 13 ♗f2! fxg3 14 hxg3 ♖xf3 15 ♗e2, with a strong attack.

13   ♖g1   *0.37*

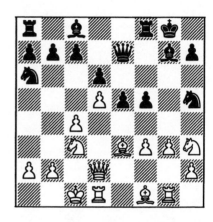

White is ready to begin his offensive on the kingside.

13   ...   **♘f6?**   *0.33*

Now the position becomes a standard one, and 9 ... ♕e7 essentially proves to be a waste of time.

Black tries to forestall White's breakthrough, but since he does not succeed in this, he should perhaps have tried to exploit the weakening of the f3 square by playing 13 ... f4. After this White has two possibilities:

(a) 14 gxf4 ♗xh3 15 ♗xh3 ♘xf4, and Black's control of f4 gives him chances of a defence.

(b) 14 ♗f2 fxg3 15 hxg3 ♖xf3
16 ♗e2 ♖xc3 17 bxc3 ♘f6. For
the sacrificed exchange Black has
adequate compensation. Thanks
to White's weakened queenside
he has quite good prospects, and
certainly better than after the
game continuation.

| 14 | ♘f2 | 0.39 | ♔h8 | 0.38 |

A prophylactic move. Black
vacates a square for his knight.

| 15 | ♗e2 | ·0.55 | | |

Of course, the immediate 15
♗g5 followed by g3-g4 was also
possible.

| 15 | ... | | ♗d7 | 0.42 |
| 16 | ♗g5 | 0.58 | ♘c5 | 1.03 |

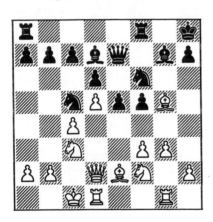

17　g4!　　0.59

After this White's offensive
develops of its own accord. Kasparov's attempts to obtain counterplay are clearly too late and
merely hasten his defeat.

17	...		e4	1.05
18	fxe4	1.02	fxe4	1.07
19	♗e3	1.08	♘a4	1.08
20	g5!	1.16	♘xc3	1.09
21	bxc3			

The weakening of White's pawns
is no longer of any significance.

21	...		♘g8	1.20
22	♘g4	1.20	c5	1.26
23	dxc6	1.33	♗xc6	1.34
24	h4	1.42		

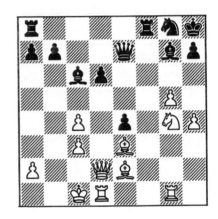

| 24 | ... | | d5 | 1.35 |

Kasparov cannot calmly watch
the white pawn advance to h6, and
he sacrifices a piece, as compensation for which he merely gains
the chance to give a 'spite' check.

25	cxd5	1.36	♗xd5	1.37
26	♕xd5		♖ac8	
27	♕d6	2.00	♖xc3+	
28	♔b1		♕f7	
29	♗d4		**Resigns**	

GAME TWENTY-FOUR   *31 December*

Thus the two players did not succeed in concluding their fifth encounter before the allotted number of games. This match, like all their preceding ones (with the exception of the terminated unlimited match) went the full distance. The concluding 24th game took place on 31 December 1990. New Year's Eve!

For the first time in the match, playing White, Kasparov avoided the king's pawn and began the game with 1 ♘f3. His choice of the English Opening was dictated by a desire to avoid sharp complications. As is well known, in the Closed Games Karpov does not employ sharp set-ups for Black. But even so, in this game Kasparov was not able completely to avoid risk.

The final game has its own rules. Remember the finale of the Seville match, when, after unpretentiously playing the opening in the 24th game and playing in positional style, Kasparov managed to snatch victory, and together with it the chess crown, from his opponent's hands. Of course, to win to order with Black in the last game is even more difficult. And yet psychological factors in a decisive encounter may prove much more important than the colour of the pieces.

Events on the board appeared to develop unhurriedly and apparently undramatically. But the nervous strain during the course of the very difficult three-month duel was bound to tell on the play of both participants. After the game Kasparov admitted that he had made a number of mistakes in the middlegame, and explained this by the enormous tension. But Karpov did not exploit the chance offered. He in turn could not withstand the tension and also made a number of serious mistakes. Kasparov gained a great material advantage and . . . offered a draw "from a position of very great strength". And Karpov, restraining his pride, extended his hand to his opponent.

That is how this most interesting and difficult match concluded. It may have set the seal on the titanic duel between the two most outstanding players of our time.

Kasparov-Karpov
English Opening

1	♘f3	0.01	♘f6	0.01
2	c4		e6	0.02
3	♘c3		♝b4	0.04

Annotating this last game of the match, which had lasted nearly three months, is not an easy matter. One might be drawn into making some judgements, guesses or suggestions. We will not do this, but will try to stick only to the facts. And the main fact was that Kasparov would be satisfied with a draw. In this case he would be the complete victor – everything would fall to him. To the title of World Champion, which he had already retained, would be added the greater part of the money prize and the special prize worth one million dollars, put up by the organisers of the Lyon half of the match.

For Karpov a win, and only a win, would enable him to share the money prize, and also to continue in a play-off for the special prize. To this one can also add the emotional factor – an honourable draw with the World Champion, and also revenge for his defeat in the last game of the match in Seville. It will be remembered that there, in the event of a draw, everything – including the title of World Champion – would have been achieved by Karpov. There

in the last game of the match Kasparov needed only a win, and he won! Thus the stakes in the present game were very high.

We will now return to the first moves of the game, and will straight away remark that the World Champion avoided here a continuation of the theoretical argument that had been a recurrent theme of the entire match. As a result of the initial moves, the position on the board is an unusual hybrid of three openings – the English Opening (of which the initial pawn move is characteristic), the Nimzo-Indian Defence, and the Queen's Indian Defence.

4	♕c2	0.02	0-0	0.09
5	a3	0.03		

Typical of Kasparov. When he has the chance to exchange a knight for an enemy bishop, he does this immediately, not worrying about the slight loss of time.

5	...		♝xc3	
6	♕xc3		b6	0.15
7	b4	0.11		

This seemingly active move in fact merely causes White difficulties. In such positions 7 b3 is preferable.

7	...		d6	0.18
8	♝b2	0.19	♝b7	0.32
9	g3	0.28	c5	0.39
10	♝g2	0.29	♘bd7	0.50
11	0-0	0.30		

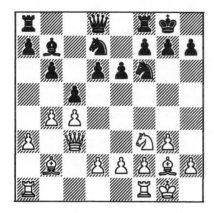

Here we can take stock. Both sides have completed the development of their minor pieces, and although White has the advantage of the two bishops, at the present moment this is not felt at all. On the other hand, Black has a lead in the deployment of his forces. He has already determined the placing of his central pawns, whereas White still has to do this. Therefore here Black should have planned what to do further, and deployed his heavy pieces in accordance with this.

11 ... ♜c8 *0.51*

A routine move! Although, in our opinion, the opening has turned out favourably for Karpov, this does not mean that his slight lead in development cannot disappear.

It is clear that Black's play may involve opening the position on the queenside, and therefore at the given moment it is far from clear which rook should stand at c8. In view of this, we would prefer the following move order: 11 ... ♛e7, ... a6 and, depending on circumstances, ... ♜fc8 and ... ♜ab8.

12 d3 *0.48* **♜e8** *0.57*

Here too 12 ... ♛e7 was preferable.

13 e4 *1.05* **a6** *1.01*

Black has finally hit on the correct plan, but precious time has been lost, and White is now ready to join battle.

14	**♛b3**	*1.18*	**b5**	*1.05*
15	**♞d2**	*1.19*	**♜b8**	*1.16*
16	**♜fc1**	*1.23*	**♝a8**	*1.20*
17	**♛d1**	*1.26*		

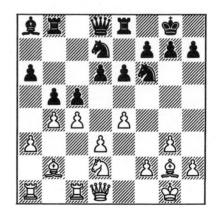

It is interesting to note how much the position has changed

during the last few moves. Black has been marking time, whereas on the queenside, where the battle will develop, White has concentrated large forces and he now has a slight initiative.

17   ...   ♕e7   *1.34*

Black finally makes this necessary and long-overdue move, and it is amazing how his forces immediately become coordinated.

18   cxb5   *1.29*   axb5   *1.35*
19   ♘b3   *1.30*

Kasparov hastens to open up the game, in order to exploit his accumulation of forces on the queenside. He succeeds in doing so, not without the assistance of his opponent.

19   ...   e5   *1.42*

It would seem that 19 ... ♖ec8 should first have been played, but after 20 ♕e2 Black cannot play 20 ... ♘b6 on account of 21 e5, while if 20 ... e5 then 21 ♗h3, and the pin is unpleasant.

20   f3!?   *1.39*

This inelegant and apparently even dubious move, which, incidentally, is typical of Kasparov (remember the second game of the match) also proves successful here. The e4 pawn is now securely defended, and the bishop, which was tied to its defence, can now carry out more appropriate attacking or defensive functions. But the obvious drawback to the move is the weakening of the g1-a7 diagonal.

20   ...   h5   *1.45*

Black could have tried to exploit this weakening immediately: 20 ... ♘b6!. After 21 bxc5 ♘a4 22 ♗c3 dxc5 23 ♗e1 a sharp situation arises, but after playing his bishop to f2 White achieves a sufficiently solid position.

21   bxc5   *1.44*   dxc5!?

It is easier for Black to defend after 21 ... ♘xc5, but he is aiming for complicated play. To be fair, it should be said there is some justification for this, and he is obliged to do so by the match situation. A sharp skirmish now develops.

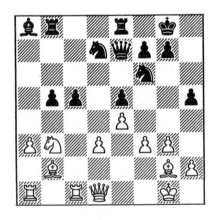

22   a4?!   *1.46*

White too does not wish to wait, and he aims to provoke an immediate crisis, but he should have been more cautious. He should have considered 22 h4, forestalling a possible attack on the kingside, or else 22 ♖c2, in order to intensify the pressure on the c-pawn.

22 ...   h4!?   *1.53*

Now 23 ... hxg3 24 hxg3 ♘h5 is threatened, when Black gains attacking chances.

23   g4   *1.57*

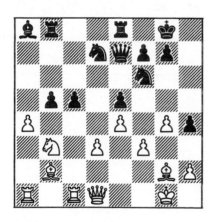

Karpov's diversion has forced the World Champion to weaken his dark squares on the kingside.

23 ...   c4?!   *1.59*

Our doubts are not caused by the fact that this move is bad. The situation on the board has changed, and Black should have transferred his hopes to the kingside. Therefore

we recommend 23 ... ♘h7 when, as can readily be seen, his initiative would have been quite dangerous for White. After 24 axb5 ♖xb5 Black holds his opponent on the queenside, and on the other flank he seizes control of the dark squares.

After the text move the centre is opened, and under such conditions a flank attack is doomed to failure.

24   dxc4   bxa4   *2.01*
25   ♗a3!   *1.59*   **♕d8**   *2.05*
26   ♘c5   *2.01*   **♗c6?**   *2.07*

One gains the impression that the Ex-World Champion had lost his head. Of course, he realised that his hopes of success had already disappeared. After the correct 26 ... ♘xc5 27 ♗xc5 ♗c6 the position is level, but it would be difficult to continue playing for a win.

27   ♘xa4   *2.03*   **♘h7**   *2.08*
28   ♘c5   *2.10*

Kasparov aims for simplification, in order to conclude the game as quickly as possible. We would remind the reader that this game was played on New Year's Eve.

28   ...   ♘g5   *2.10*
29   ♘xd7   *2.11*   **♗xd7**
30   ♖c3!   *2.12*

By defending the third rank, White deprives his opponent of his last hope of at least complicating the game. As a result, another mistake by Karpov follows.

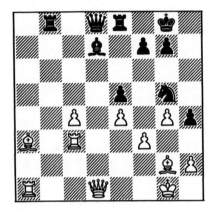

30   ...   ♛a5?   2.19

This loses material. Black should have played 30 ... ♞e6, when he retains compensation for the sacrificed pawn on account of White's weakened kingside.

31   ♖d3   2.14   ♗a4

The bishop was attacked, and both 32 ♗d6 and 32 ♗e7 were also threatened.

32   ♛e1   2.15   ♛a6   2.26

Karpov did not want to exchange queens, but after . . .

33	♗c1!	2.17	♞e6	2.27
34	♖da3	2.18	♞c5	
35	♗e3	2.19	♛d6	2.28
36	♖xa4			

. . . White won two pieces for a rook, and offered a **draw**, which was accepted.

PROGRESSIVE SCORES

Game No.	1	2	3	4	5	6	7	8	9	10	11	12
	½	1½	2	2½	3	3½	3½	4	4½	5	5½	6
Kasparov	½	1	½	½	½	½	0	½	½	½	½	½
Karpov	½	0	½	½	½	½	1	½	½	½	½	½
	½	½	1	1½	2	2½	3½	4	4½	5	5½	6

Game No.	13	14	15	16	17	18	19	20	21	22	23	24
	6½	7	7½	8½	8½	9½	10	11	11½	12	12	12½
Kasparov	½	½	½	1	0	1	½	1	½	½	0	½
Karpov	½	½	½	0	1	0	½	0	½	½	1	½
	6½	7	7½	7½	8½	8½	9	9	9½	10	11	11½

Index of Openings

References are to game numbers